"When I lived in Virginia, I got to know Chris Sicks and the people of Alexandria Presbyterian Church. What I saw and experienced through their ministry was Christ's grace 'with skin on.' Now that I train seminary students, I gladly pass along Chris's clear description of the place of mercy in gospel ministry, not only because his reasons are biblical but because God's mercy is real in his life."

—GREG PERRY, associate professor of New Testament and director of the City Ministry Initiative, Covenant Seminary, Saint Louis

"Lots of us have been waiting for a fresh voice to shine renewed light on the old, tired evangelistic debate between words and deeds. Thank God for *Tangible*! You will be encouraged and moved to action as I was."

—BISHOP TODD HUNTER, professor; author of *Christianity Beyond Belief*

"Because of our emphasis on God's grace, Christians rarely appreciate the value of goodness for both human thriving and the extension of the mission of Jesus in the world. *Tangible* provides clear biblical understanding of the meaning and implications of goodness. Time to catch up!"

—ALAN HIRSCH, author, activist, and dreamer

"Our faith is based on God's mercy, so the best way to draw others to faith is to show His mercy working through our deeds. In this book, Chris Sicks shows a wonderful grasp of Scripture and demonstrates how a biblical pattern can be reflected in our witness for Christ."

—DR. JOHN FRAME, professor of systematic theology and philosophy, Reformed Theological Seminary

"In a world full of physical and spiritual poverty, *Tangible* encourages us toward a life and ministry of mercy that affirms the reality and authenticity of Jesus. This book is for anyone who yearns to lead the way to Jesus, who addresses all of our needs."

—CARRIE BROWN, divisional training coordinator, Young Life International

"Chris Sicks makes a compelling case for an apologetic combining ministry in word and deed. He reminds us that the church must embody what the world needs: gospel show-and-tell, the living Christ, offered in grace and truth."

—AL LACOUR, coordinator, Reformed University Fellowship International

"Just as faith without works is dead, proper theology without a proper response is inadequate. In his insightful and challenging new book, Chris Sicks discusses how a proper understanding of theology leads to a proper response."

—MARK A. GREEN, president, White Horse Inn

TANGIBLE

MAKING GOD KNOWN THROUGH
DEEDS OF MERCY AND WORDS OF TRUTH

CHRIS SICKS

NAVPRESS
Discipleship Inside Out®

NAVPRESS

Discipleship Inside Out®

NavPress is the publishing ministry of The Navigators, an international Christian organization and leader in personal spiritual development. NavPress is committed to helping people grow spiritually and enjoy lives of meaning and hope through personal and group resources that are biblically rooted, culturally relevant, and highly practical.

For a free catalog go to www.NavPress.com
or call 1.800.366.7788 in the United States or 1.800.839.4769 in Canada.

ISBN-13: 978-1-61291-441-1

Cover design by Faceout Studio, Jeff Miller
Cover image by Shutterstock

Some of the anecdotal illustrations in this book are true to life and are included with the permission of the persons involved. All other illustrations are composites of real situations, and any resemblance to people living or dead is coincidental.

Unless otherwise identified, all Scripture quotations in this publication are taken from the Holy Bible, English Standard Version (ESV), copyright © 2001 by Crossway, a publishing ministry of Good News Publishers. ESV® Text Edition: 2011. Used by permission. All rights reserved. Other versions used include: the *Holy Bible, New International Version*® (NIV®), copyright © 1973, 1978, 1984, 2011 by Biblica, Inc.®, used by permission of Zondervan, all rights reserved worldwide. The "NIV" and "New International Version" are trademarks registered in the United States Patent and Trademark Office by Biblica, Inc.®; and the King James Version (KJV).

Cataloging-in-Publication Data is available.

Printed in the United States of America

1 2 3 4 5 6 7 8 / 18 17 16 15 14 13

Elijah took the child and brought him down from the upper chamber into the house and delivered him to his mother. And Elijah said, "See, your son lives." And the woman said to Elijah, "Now I know that you are a man of God, and that the word of the Lord in your mouth is truth."

1 Kings 17:23-24

They shall speak of the glory of your kingdom and tell of your power, to make known to the children of man your mighty deeds, and the glorious splendor of your kingdom.

Psalm 145:11-12

CONTENTS

FOREWORD

At the beginning of Jesus' ministry, He stood up in the synagogue at Nazareth and declared that He was the fulfillment of these words of Isaiah: "The Spirit of the Lord is upon me, because he has anointed me to proclaim good news to the poor. He has sent me to proclaim liberty to the captives and recovering of sight to the blind, to set at liberty those who are oppressed, to proclaim the year of the Lord's favor" (Luke 4:18-19). In this declaration and in His ministry Jesus showed that bringing freedom for captives and relief to the poor and oppressed are at the very center of His divine mission. His ultimate act of liberation was His sinless life, substitutionary death, and victorious resurrection, which set His people free from slavery to sin and death. Yet His teachings and example show us that if the gospel message is to be recognized in its full power, the proclamation of the good news of Christ's saving work should be accompanied by tangible acts of love, service, and mercy toward our neighbors.

Historically, the Christian church has at its best been known for exemplary love and sacrificial service to "the least of these"—the poor, oppressed, and marginalized. Such service has provided a powerful apologetic for the gospel. The fourth-century church provides one example:

> In his attempt to reestablish Hellenic religion in the empire, [the emperor] Julian instructed the high priest of the Hellenic faith to imitate Christian concern for strangers. . . . He therefore instructed the priest to establish hostels for needy strangers in every city and also ordered a distribution of corn and wine to the poor, strangers, and beggars. "For it is disgraceful that, when no Jew ever has to beg, and the impious Galileans [Christians] support not only their own poor but ours as well, all men see that our people lack aid from us. Teach those of the Hellenic faith to contribute to public service of this sort."[1]

In more recent history, Christian churches of the eighteenth and nineteenth centuries led the charge for the abolition of slavery, again providing a strong apologetic for the Christian faith and visibly embodying Jesus' mission to proclaim liberty to captives.

Mercy ministry is an opportunity for Christian churches to take the gospel to those most in need, provide the marginalized and oppressed an alternative community centered on Jesus (the church), and show the transformative power of the gospel to the watching world. Moreover, responding to social injustice in our communities is a way the church can practice the charge of Jeremiah 29:7 for God's people to seek the welfare of the cities where God has placed us, and to obey the call of James to practice "pure religion" (James 1:27) by caring for the most vulnerable.

Chris Sicks knows firsthand that mercy ministry is an effective apologetic for the gospel. A former atheist who rejected many intellectual apologetic arguments, Chris is now a pastor who leads numerous mercy ministry initiatives. He has seen with his own eyes how God uses the church to both help hurting people and to reveal Himself to them and others. In the midst of their suffering, people need to see God as Rescuer, Healer, Comforter, and Savior. Thousands of Christians are already serving the poor and oppressed, and many are also committed to the work of apologetics. Sicks' intent is to help the church see how deeds of compassion can be a compelling argument for the existence of a loving God.

Chris is not promoting a repackaged Social Gospel. He understands that the gospel cannot be communicated through deeds alone; as Duane Litfin has written, "If it is to be communicated at all, the gospel must be put into words."[2] In this book, Chris repeatedly emphasizes that deeds of mercy are insufficient in themselves, and do not by themselves form an apologetic. Instead, the combination of deeds of mercy and words of salvation comprise what Chris has called the *apologetic of mercy*.[3]

Most apologetic strategies target the head. In contrast, the apologetic of mercy begins with the heart. It is often in the midst of our pain that the "God of all comfort" makes Himself known most clearly. This is not a new idea, but it is the pattern of God's gracious interaction with His people in the Old and New Testaments, and continues in His dealings with us today.

God has placed each of us in a particular place, in relationships with people who have needs. If we ask Him to use us to reveal Himself, we will have the privilege of showing His compassion and love to hurting people. As we make meals, give rides, or provide shelter, we will build relationships. When we share the gospel in the context of a merciful relationship, we speak with authenticity. Our words *about* God's love are believable because we have *shown* God's love in action and in truth (see 1 John 3:18).

Justin Holcomb
Director of The Resurgence
Pastor at Mars Hill Church, Seattle, Washington

PART I

THE APOLOGETIC OF MERCY: *WHY*

Let your light shine before others, so that they may see your good works and give glory to your Father who is in heaven.

Matthew 5:16

Jesus of Nazareth, a man who was a prophet mighty in deed and word before God and all the people.

Luke 24:19

I will cause you to be inhabited as in your former times, and will do more good to you than ever before. **Then you will know** that I am the LORD.

Ezekiel 36:11

CHAPTER 1

TANGIBLE GRACE

The kingdom of God is the structure of reality. . . . It is the church's purpose to keep this threatened, difficult-to-believe kingdom of God constantly before people's eyes.[1]

DALE BRUNER

When he graduated from college, John Meinen was a Zen Buddhist with a heart for serving the poor. A "poster child for postmodern relativism," John believed that morality is culturally conditioned, that people are inherently good, and that the world is an illusion. Then he went to Bangladesh.

"The beggars pulling on my clothes were no illusion," John says. After four months of studying how microenterprise might help the poor, he left Bangladesh shaken. He had seen too many oppressed people oppressing one another to believe that people are inherently good. His youthful optimism was gone: "When I left Bangladesh, Dhaka was under siege. Jostled in the backseat of a rickshaw on my way to the airport, I saw cars being smashed, people being bloodied, and smoke billowing on the horizon. My heart was broken. My head was spinning. My world was falling apart."

A few months later, John was in Nairobi. Unemployed with little to do, he had accepted an invitation to work with a sports outreach organization. One day he was following his guide, a poor local man. They came upon a small child rummaging in the trash. John's guide suddenly scooped up the homeless boy and held him, speaking gently to him.

Time out, John thought. *Why would this man, who is suffering himself, pick up this child and enter into a world of even more suffering? How does someone do that?* Why *would someone do that?* The selfless love this man showed was an affront to John's conscience.

So John asked him why he had reached out to help the child. The man said, "I love Jesus."

"I'm not proud to say it, but I kind of laughed," John says. "I thought it was a trite answer. *You love Jesus?* Give me a break."

But in that village John witnessed many tangible acts of love: impoverished women praying for their neighbors, people in the slums serving and loving one another, and men and women with insufficient resources sharing the little they had with one another.

When he saw these deeds of mercy, John wanted to know more about the motivation behind them. He asked people, "Why do you *do* that? What enables you to love like that?" Again and again, their reply was "I love Jesus." John says, "I realized I didn't know who Jesus was, but I had to meet Him."

John and Jesus did meet. They now know one another well, because the all-powerful God of the universe revealed Himself to one young man on the streets of Bangladesh and in the slums of Africa. John saw love in transformed people, and then met the Source of that love. Today as an ordained campus minister at the University of Vermont, John tells college students about that Source.

Two thousand years ago, another man named John wrote about other-centered love and how it testifies to God's existence: "No one has ever seen God; but if we love one another, God lives in us and his love is made complete in us" (1 John 4:12, NIV).

The invisible God continues to reveal Himself to people today in very visible ways. When God's children pour out love and compassion into the lives of hurting and broken people, we declare, "Yes! There is a God! Despite all the data to the contrary in this broken world, there really is a Rescuer in heaven, and He cares about your suffering, your sadness, and your soul."

"DEED PEOPLE" AND "WORD PEOPLE"

Many of God's people are moved to serve the poor, imprisoned, and persecuted. Wonderful. Deeds of mercy for the hurting bring God glory and please Him greatly, because God is merciful (see Jeremiah 9:23-24; Micah 6:8). I call this group of believers "deed people."

Others feel the urgent need for people to know Christ, so they focus on evangelism and apologetics. Wonderful. Words of truth must be proclaimed so everyone will hear and understand the good news about our Savior (see Romans 10:14-17). I call this group "word people."

Too often word people and deed people are suspicious and critical of one another. Sometimes their critique is warranted— when word people abandon deed ministry entirely, or when deed people don't call people to repentance. When those things happen, we truncate the gospel message and our efforts suffer. The church must both *demonstrate* and *declare* God's compassion for bodies and souls. That's what the early church did, following Jesus' example.[2]

Alone in prison, John the Baptist began to question whether the man he had called the Lamb of God was really the Messiah. He had been convinced of it not long before. That was when "all of Jerusalem" was coming out to hear John preach. Later, sitting in a cell before his execution, John began to doubt. (Wouldn't you?) John sent a message to Jesus: "Are you the one who is to come, or shall we look for another?" (Luke 7:19).

What was Jesus' response? Did He reply with a carefully worded apologetic argument? Or a philosophical essay proving His identity? No, He said, "Go and tell John what you have seen and heard: the blind receive their sight, the lame walk, lepers are cleansed, and the deaf hear, the dead are raised up, the poor have good news preached to them" (verse 22). Jesus said His deeds of mercy were proof that He was for real. His loving actions were tangible grace. They authenticated the message of the gospel He preached.

Mercy and truth came together in the person of Jesus Christ (see Psalm 85:10-11; John 1:14) and continue to do so today, in His body. Through us, God is continuing to expand His kingdom of righteousness, peace, and healing into the dark places of the world. Believers involved in holistic ministry are on the front lines of this advancing kingdom because *knowledge of God is found at the intersection of human need and divine sufficiency.*

THE APOLOGETIC OF MERCY

In this book I am proposing an *apologetic of mercy.* This approach combines word and deed ministry in a way that is persuasive. The combination is effective, and biblical, because it acknowledges the variety of human needs.

We often think of needy people as those who lack material things. But people are complex. Everyone has emotional, spiritual, relational, and material needs. Each of these needs impacts the others.[3] Ministry is less compassionate, less effective, when it addresses one type of needs but ignores the others.

Human needs are the lens through which people can see God. We help hurting people focus that lens on Him when we tell them, "I know God may seem distant from you now, or nonexistent. But there truly is a Rescuer in heaven. He cares about your suffering, your sadness, and your soul. In fact, He sent me here to help you — and to tell you all about Him." God actually uses us, the body of Christ, as part of His self-revelation.

Throughout the Bible, God reveals *who He is* at the exact point of *what people need.* The whole story of Scripture is one of

God rescuing people in tangible ways and thereby making Himself known to them. God shows people who He is by answering their calls for help.

In the book of Exodus God says,

NEED

Moreover, I have heard the *groaning* of the Israelites, whom the Egyptians are *enslaving*, and I have remembered my covenant.

RESPONSE

Therefore, say to the Israelites: "I am the LORD, and *I will bring you* out from under the yoke of the Egyptians. *I will free you* from being slaves to them, and *I will redeem you* with an outstretched arm and with mighty acts of judgment. *I will take you* as my own people, and *I will be your God*.

KNOWLEDGE

Then you will know that I am the LORD your God, who brought you out from under the yoke of the Egyptians." (6:5-7, NIV, emphasis added)

God says He is *aware* of Israel's suffering. He isn't a distant, impersonal god. He is the covenantal God of Abraham who sees the Israelites' need and remembers His promise from Genesis 15. Then, God promises to address Israel's needs in five ways: *"I will bring you. . . . I will free you. . . . I will redeem you. . . . I will take you. . . . I will be your God."* Each of those actions leads to God's main purpose: relationship. He says that through His deeds of compassion, *the Israelites will know* that

He is the Lord, their God. They will see and know Him through His saving acts.[4]

God's people had emotional, spiritual, relational, and material needs. God responded in word and deed so that the Israelites would have a relationship with Him. Today, billions of people have those same emotional, spiritual, relational, and material needs. God calls us, His children, whom He has already served, to imitate His ministry—using deeds of mercy and words of truth. We do it to make His grace visible and lead people to Christ. Need for Him is what every other need points to.

WHAT LIES AHEAD

In the first part of the book we'll explore more deeply what the apologetic of mercy is, with an eye for why making grace tangible is so essential. In part 2 we'll look at how to put the apologetic of mercy into practice.

If you are committed to evangelism and sharing the gospel verbally, I encourage you to keep an open mind as we look at how merciful deeds can open the hearts of your audience to the good news you speak. Jesus came to relieve the burdens of pain and death, not simply to answer our questions. He didn't come here to show that He *exists*, but that He is *Savior*. God's people need to proclaim the gospel, and also work hard to provide tangible evidence that this gospel is true—that God actually cares.

If you are committed to deeds of mercy, I challenge you to always speak the words of the gospel and to pray with those you help. We do no lasting good unless we recognize that every person has a soul that needs Christ.[5] Don't assume that people understand the connection between your Christian faith and the mercy you offer. Be sure to tell them about the Source of your love and how they can know Him.

God can use you, right where you are with the resources you have, to help people experience His mercy now and know Him forever.

(Note: To get the most out of this book, don't just skim over the Scripture references in each chapter and in the endnotes. I'm not making this stuff up. These principles come from the Word of God, not my head. God's words are authoritative and mine are not. Take the time to look up the referenced passages and let God speak to you through them.)

QUESTIONS FOR REFLECTION OR DISCUSSION

1. What are the emotional, spiritual, relational, and material needs in your life?
2. In what ways has God met your needs? Why is it important to be conscious of your own neediness before you try to serve others?
3. Are you more of a deed person or a word person? Why?
4. In your church, can you discern an emphasis on either word or deed ministry? If your church does both, how connected are they to one another?

CHAPTER 2

TELL *AND* SHOW: DEEDS AUTHENTICATE THE MESSAGE

*Then they cried to the L*ORD *in their trouble, and he delivered them from their distress. He sent out his word and healed them, and delivered them from their destruction.*

PSALM 107:19-20

Let us not love in word or talk but in deed and in truth.

1 JOHN 3:18

Bill Monroe invented bluegrass music. The style is named after his band, the Blue Grass Boys. Because television, magazines, and the Internet carry their images everywhere, today's music stars are easy to recognize. But that was not the case for Monroe, who was born in 1911. For much of his sixty-year career he was known by his music, not his face.

One night in the 1980s, Monroe rushed onto the tour bus

at two or three in the morning and woke the band. His banjo player, Blake Williams, heard Monroe shout, "Hurry, you all get your music and come inside, quick!"[1]

The sleepy Blue Grass Boys found themselves outside a truck stop. Once inside, the band pulled out their instruments and played "Uncle Pen" and "Blue Moon of Kentucky" for a small crowd of skeptics in the truck stop restaurant. Then, Bill pointed to a customer and said, "See, I *told* you I'm Bill Monroe!"

How did Monroe persuade a group of nonbelievers that he was who he claimed to be? He didn't argue with them or debate the issue. Bill Monroe did more than *tell* the skeptics who he was; he showed them.[2]

REMOVING OBSTACLES TO FAITH

Have you ever read this verse in the Bible?

> Come, everyone who questions, come to the classroom;
> and he who has no answers, come and understand!
> Come, buy textbooks and journal articles without
> money and without price.

Or this one?

> Come to me all you who are doubtful and full of
> skepticism,
> and I will give you carefully constructed defenses of my
> existence.

No, the Bible does not seem to be written for the skeptic as much as for the sufferer. Skeptics may certainly find answers in God's Word, which is "living and active, sharper than any two-edged sword" (Hebrews 4:12). Yet, over and over in the Bible, God doesn't argue with skeptics. He shows up in person and rescues them.[3] When the Son of God came to earth in the flesh He told weary, hungry, fearful, heavy-laden people, "Come to Me." His very presence was the ultimate apologetic argument.

If you've ever tried to persuade someone to believe in Jesus, you've engaged in apologetics. The work of apologetics is to remove obstacles to a person's faith. Traditionally, apologetics has attempted to answer intellectual doubts. It is word ministry. One person uses words to persuade another to believe that God exists and Christ is our Savior. According to Douglas Groothuis, "Christian apologetics is the rational defense of the Christian worldview as objectively true, rationally compelling and existentially or subjectively engaging."[4] This kind of apologetics is often effective among people with intellectual or philosophical doubts.

But many other people—perhaps *most* people in the world today—face other obstacles to faith: Pain. Hardship. Suffering. Persecution. They are not interested in an intellectual argument for the existence of God, because they are too distracted by their child's illness, the lack of clean water, or their poverty and oppression. They will probably have a hard time believing that God is compassionate until we show them some compassion.

Our message about God's compassion will lack credibility if we preach to people's minds and ignore the pain in their bodies and hearts (see James 2:15-16). If we begin instead with people's emotional and material needs, we open the door to talk about their spiritual and relational needs. Yes, we must testify to the character and nature of God—we must proclaim the gospel—but sometimes it is best to start with deeds rather than words. To show first, and then tell.

A BROADER DEFINITION

The apologetic of mercy could be considered an extension of the moral argument for the existence of God, which says the very existence of universal moral codes and humanity's efforts to comply prove there is a God. A philosopher may bat this moral argument back and forth as an intellectual pastime, but a struggling single mother does not want to play along. Intellect isn't her problem; it is her gas bill, her stress, her loneliness, and her fear. We should tell her about Jesus, of course, but we should first do something about her pain. The merciful apologist steps into her life, addresses her physical burdens, soothes her emotional scars, and then presents Christ as the answer to her heart's pain.

The moral argument defends the existence of God as an idea. The apologetic of mercy puts ideas into action. It combines deeds and words to impact the heart, not just the head. It is the moral argument brought to life, made incarnate—in *your* flesh. When you do acts of mercy *and* proclaim the words of the gospel, you are making the moral argument in both word and deed. The apologetic of mercy isn't cool, detached, and academic. It gets down on a person's level to address the mind, heart, and body in a persuasive way.

Thinking of apologetics and evangelism in this way can help us approach anyone in the world today. For instance, people who have intellectual doubts need to hear rational answers that address their doubts. They should learn why it is reasonable to believe God exists, became human, suffered, and then died to save sinners. However, a person with significant material needs needs for us to first address those needs.

It is Christ alone who saves, of course. But He puts us in the battle at the places where brokenness and healing meet. We are field medics who bring mercy to the wounded, carrying not only material resources to address physical needs, but also the message of the gospel that revives souls.[5] As we bandage and feed broken bodies, we speak words of truth and pray that God will reveal Himself to broken hearts and doubting minds. That combination forms the apologetic of mercy.

A TANGIBLE SIGN OF THE DIVINE PRESENCE

Several years ago, our church had the opportunity to sponsor the asylum application of a young man from Burundi. Guy Seshaka had to flee his country because his Tutsi family had become a target of the Hutu government, which didn't like the things Guy's father, a journalist, was writing. A young lawyer in our church invested two hundred pro bono hours into building Guy's case for political asylum. Curt did a great job and persuaded the judge to grant Guy asylum so he could join the church that had supported and encouraged him for nine months while he was held in detention.

After telling Guy the good news, the judge turned to me and said, "I would like to commend your church for its commitment to this young man, and for your faithfulness to the gospel message." I'm not sure if federal immigration judges normally talk like that, but this one had seen the gospel at work, the connection between word and deed.

And he wasn't the only one. When Guy fled Burundi, he was already a Christian. His father was not. His broad intellect was one stumbling block. The genocide he had witnessed was another. But his heart was changed when he saw the work of God in his son's life. He wrote to us:

> I live in a country which has been torn apart by wars and violence on a horrifying scale. The unspeakable atrocities I have witnessed pushed me to draw the conclusion that God had quit our planet and was no longer mindful of our collective plight. Ladies and gentlemen of Alexandria Presbyterian Church, you have proved me otherwise. And, hand on heart, I confess that I have been mistaken and that my pessimistic conclusion has been hasty. Definitely, God is still very much around and is overseeing every human undertaking. Your church is a visible sign of the divine presence in the world.

God has not abandoned the world. He uses the body of Christ as a "visible sign of the divine presence in the world."

Guy's father had heard the gospel. He understood the truth claims of Christianity—in his head. As a journalist, he's the sort of guy who would enjoy intellectual sparring with a professor of apologetics. But scholars don't make the best witnesses in a hurting world. Doubt arises in our hearts as often as our heads. The path to faith for Guy's father began in his heart rather than his head.

Guy's father is now a believer in Christ, because the claims of Christianity were made tangible in the life of his son. As Francis Schaeffer said so well,

> The final apologetic, along with the rational, logical defense and presentation, is *what the world sees* in the individual Christian and in our corporate relationships together. . . . What we are called to do, upon the basis of the finished work of Christ in the power of the Spirit through faith, is to exhibit a substantial healing, individual and corporate, so that people may observe it. This too is a portion of the apologetic: a presentation that gives at least some demonstration that these things are not theoretical but real; not perfect, yet substantial. If we only speak of and exhibit the individual effects of the gospel, the world, psychologically conditioned as it is today, will explain them away. What the world cannot explain away will be substantial, corporate exhibition of the logical conclusions of the Christian presuppositions.[6]

SEEING IS BELIEVING

I find it fascinating that Jesus chose to help hurting people as the most frequent proof of His divinity. He could have commanded the sky to rain or snow, moved mountains, and turned rocks into diamonds. These acts would have demonstrated His divinity as clearly as healing and feeding did. He once calmed a storm on the Sea of Galilee, but even then His attention was on the terrified men in the boat. Jesus' heart of compassion was always moved by people and their needs.

God loves to heal the needy and broken because as Creator He remembers what creation looked like before the Fall. Jesus remembers a time when there was no death, no leprosy, and no blindness. He came to restore that state of affairs, to erase the consequences of the Fall and put things right. His sacrificial death was the ultimate deed of mercy, and it taught us the true meaning of love (see 1 John 3:16-18).

People search high and low for love and for relief from their heart's pain, unaware it is God they really seek. "The young man who rings the bell at the brothel is unconsciously looking for God."[7] Every hurting person who cries out "Why?" unconsciously asks that question to God.

A few years ago, Tammy sat in my office and told me about her problems. She was living in her Ford Explorer with her four children. She took the three oldest to school each day, the baby to a friend's house. Then she went to one of her two jobs. She told me that when she was sixteen her mother died. Her father drove down to North Carolina to pick up an aunt and uncle for the funeral, and on the way back they were all killed in a car accident. So this sixteen-year-old only child had to bury her mother, father, aunt, and uncle in one weekend. In the twenty years since, there had been little joy or success in Tammy's life.

She asked me, "Why did that happen to us? My mom went to church every week; my family were good people. Why didn't God take someone else?"

What would you say to someone like Tammy? How would you respond? Would you try to explain the inscrutable will of God? (Let me know how that works for you.)

If you are a "word ministry" person, here's an important thing to recognize: Tammy wasn't only asking, "Why, God?" she was also asking, "Where are You, God?" Situations like this are opportunities to teach someone about the character of the Lord, to teach that He is merciful — *not as an academic theory, but as a present reality.*

So here's what I did: I loved her. I listened and prayed, but waited to address her questions until a better time. Instead of giving Tammy answers for her head, I gave her hope for her heart. I worked with the deacons and members of our church to provide Tammy with food and clothes for the children. We helped them find a place to live. And, then, because Tammy is a whole person who also needs Jesus, we read Scripture with her, prayed with her, and explained the gospel. We used words and shared the Word of God. But first we showed her tangible compassion. We did not ignore her questions; we just waited to answer until Tammy had concrete evidence of God's love for her. The fact that God actually did care about her on this earth made it easier for her to believe He cared about her soul in eternity.

COMPLETE LOVE

The skeptical crowd at that truck stop didn't believe Bill Monroe was who he said he was—initially. He was known by his music, so that's how he revealed his identity. The audience believed only when they saw his hands play the music. We would do well to remember this when we try to reveal God to those who don't know Him.

Just as those skeptics didn't know Bill Monroe's face, neither does anyone know God's face. No matter which awful Jesus painting we may have seen in our Sunday school classroom, it wasn't a portrait of Him. So, how will people recognize God today? According to the apostle John, one of the most recognizable things about God is His love. And we have a role to play in revealing that love: "Dear friends, since God so loved us, we also ought to love one another. No one has ever seen God; but if we love one another, God lives in us and his love is made complete in us" (1 John 4:11-12, NIV).

You see what John is saying, right? Not that God's love is incomplete without us, but that, in some mysterious way, we bring the love of God to complete fulfillment when it is visible, tangible, reflected—in us. John tells us, in effect, "No one can see God's face. Jesus isn't here physically anymore. But when we love one another, we reveal God's loving character. The invisible God becomes visible through our love."[8]

Millions of nonbelievers have heard the claim "Jesus loves

you." Many will dismiss those words until God's people match them with compassionate deeds. When they see us perform deeds of love, our words will become far more convincing.

SUMMARY

"Word people" often use apologetic methods to defend the truth claims of Christianity against philosophical objections. That can work well in an academic setting. But much of the world is too racked with physical and emotional pain to worry about metaphysics and epistemology. Only a small percentage of people even know what those words mean!

We will have more impact if we remember what John Calvin wrote: "The heart's distrust is greater than the mind's blindness."[9] Pain and suffering cause human hearts to distrust God, or to disbelieve entirely. The apologetic of mercy calls the body of Christ to respond to these needs with love, comfort, and help. If we do, we can effectively persuade distrusting hearts that God is real and worthy of trust. The apologetic of mercy addresses needs in a comprehensive way, just as Jesus did, declaring to hurting people that God cares not only for their souls, but also for their material needs.

Billions of people struggle with fear, despair, poverty, loneliness, guilt, and persecution. That is the context of their lives. Don't be guilty of drive-by evangelism. Slow down. Stop. Love. Listen. Use more than words. Embody the love and compassion you speak of, and your words will be far more credible. God loves to use His people to address both physical and spiritual needs—just as He always has.

QUESTIONS FOR REFLECTION OR DISCUSSION

1. Name some things you have filled your heart with, other than God.
2. When you became a believer in Jesus, would you say it was primarily a change in your heart or in your head? Did one come first? Explain your answer.
3. When has the body of Christ met your needs? How did that experience affect your faith?
4. What tangible things can you do to meet people's needs with the resources God has given you? Who could you bless in those tangible ways?

CHAPTER 3

SHOW *AND* TELL: WORDS ARTICULATE THE MESSAGE

The answer to everyone's question is the gospel. Ministry is spending enough time with people to help them figure out what question they are asking.[1]

FRED HARRELL

And whatever you do, in word or deed, do everything in the name of the Lord Jesus, giving thanks to God the Father through him.

COLOSSIANS 3:17

After the terrorist attacks of September 11, 2001, people around the country sent money to our denomination's headquarters to help those in New York and Washington, DC, affected by the attacks. I was asked to find people in the DC area we could help with these funds.

I quickly learned that families of the people killed in the attacks were getting assistance from many sources. Even if we wanted to help those families, no one would give me their contact information. Then I read in the paper that many big conferences had been canceled in the DC area, and thousands of tourists were changing their vacation plans. Many were afraid to visit the nation's capital. As a result, hotel bookings plummeted.

Before 9/11, the Hotel Employees International Union Local 25 had eight thousand members working in hotels and restaurants in the DC area. Because the attacks affected hotel and restaurant business so severely, four thousand members of Local 25 were laid off or let go. Every day, about a hundred of them went to the union office, asking for help.

Jorge Rivera was my contact at the office. He said his members really needed food, so we purchased $2,000 in grocery gift cards as a first step. "But," I told Jorge, "we would like you to give two things to each person who receives a gift card: A note telling them that the food was a gift from the Lord and an expression of Christ's love. We also want you to give them a Bible." Jorge agreed, so I took the food cards to him along with Bibles in English, Spanish, Portuguese, French, Amharic, and Korean—languages spoken by many members of Local 25.

Jorge told me later that he thought the Bibles were an unnecessary waste of time. By his own admission, Jorge was a nonbeliever who hadn't set foot in a church in decades. But, he thought, *My people need food. If I have to give out these folks' Bibles to get them some food, I'm willing to do that.*

Jorge was shocked by what happened. He told me that each person received the food cards and told him thank you. But when he handed them Bibles in their own language, many of them grabbed a Bible, clutched it to their chest, and said, "Thank you! *This* is what I have really needed!"

"These were hungry people," Jorge said. "Why were they so excited about a book when food was what they really needed?" I told him my theory: because their physical hunger had exposed their spiritual hunger.

PHYSICAL NEEDS EXPOSE SPIRITUAL HUNGER

If you are a "deed" person, this is something you must remember: Physical needs are tied to spiritual needs. God loves us so much that He will even *put* physical needs in our lives in order to call our attention to our need for Him. God had His people wander in a desert for forty years so they might realize they needed Him more than food itself: "[God] humbled you and let you hunger and fed you with manna . . . that he might make you know that man does not live by bread alone, but man lives by every word that comes from the mouth of the LORD" (Deuteronomy 8:3).

Moses said God humbled *you* (Israel), but then said *every* person is dependent upon God. Whether we acknowledge it or not, every one of us depends upon "every word" from the Lord—for life itself, and for the things we enjoy in life. Sometimes, however, we enjoy those things so much that we think they are all we need. We forget who made them, who made us, and who wants to be our Father for all time.

Those members of Union Local 25 needed food. Our church could have simply given them food. Their circumstances would have improved for a week or two. But Jesus didn't die on the cross to better our circumstances. He died to save our souls. That's why we asked Jorge to pass out Bibles—the Bread of Life—along with the food cards. It required more work on our part, and Jorge thought it odd. Yet, if we serve a person's earthly body and neglect his or her eternal soul, it is like treating a cancer patient with aspirin. It helps the pain but ignores the real problem.

THE MOST FUNDAMENTAL HUMAN NEED

The most fundamental human need is salvation. Our broken relationship with God is the ache that lurks behind every other pain. Even when He provides physical blessings, God is always drawing us into relationship. Ministry done in His name should do the same.

Every day in the Sinai Desert, God rained bread from heaven upon the children of Israel. Still, they complained to Moses that they were tired of being out in the desert, and they were getting tired of bread. Listen to what God said to Moses: "I have heard the grumbling of the Israelites. Tell them, 'At twilight you will eat meat, and in the morning you will be filled with bread. *Then you will know* that I am the LORD your God'" (Exodus 16:11-12, NIV, emphasis added).

It would not surprise us at all if verse 12 read, "You will be filled with bread, then you will *be satisfied*." The people did eat, of course, and they were satisfied. But according to God, there was a more important outcome: *knowledge of Him*. Knowledge of God is even more important than food. A full stomach lasts a few hours. A relationship with God lasts forever.

Which is why loving deeds are not enough. We cannot communicate the gospel through actions alone. "Repent and believe" are not things we can "say" through deeds. If it is possible to "preach" the gospel through deeds alone, then the Red Cross is preaching the gospel. Deeds of mercy that do not point to the Source of mercy are not complete gospel ministry.[2] We proclaim Jesus Himself as the *end*, not as the *means* to better circumstances. The true gospel comes from Jesus Christ and leads people to Jesus Christ.

Every human being will spend eternity either with God or without Him.[3] Can you name something more important than that? You cannot, which is why the church has always been devoted to preaching the gospel, and not through deeds alone.[4] Evangelism is inherently a verbal activity: "Jesus came into Galilee, *proclaiming* the gospel of God, and *saying*, 'The time is fulfilled, and the kingdom of God is at hand; repent and believe in the gospel'" (Mark 1:14-15, emphasis added).

We must do more than proclaim the gospel with words, of course, as we saw in the last chapter. If we ignore the felt needs of our neighbors God will charge us with disobedience, as Scripture makes abundantly clear.[5] At the same time, if we ignore the spiritual hunger of our neighbors we fail to communicate the whole gospel. The apologetic of mercy is the combination of both word and deed ministry.

POINTING PEOPLE TO CHRIST

If you are on the highway and read, "Burger King: 2 miles ahead," you don't immediately pull over, do you? Why not?

Because the sign isn't the thing you seek; it points you to that thing. The apostle John described the supernatural deeds of Jesus as *signs* rather than miracles. This is more significant than you might think.

John did not want to emphasize the miraculous things Christ did; he wanted to highlight who He was. The signs Jesus performed pointed back to Him, revealing Him as the one complete solution for human needs. Our need for purification, for relationship, for healing, for nourishment—all are met in Christ.

People's needs get their attention, forcing them to hunt for signs of hope and relief. As believers, we should address people's needs, whether we do so by giving a homeless person shelter or an elderly neighbor a ride to the grocery store. Such tangible expressions of love build friendships and trust. As we create relationships with people we can talk with them about their eternal needs. For example, we can tell the homeless person that the shelter we provide for the body is a sign that homeless hearts can take shelter in God. When we befriend a lonely neighbor we can also tell him or her about the Friend who will never leave us. As we make the grace of God tangible through gracious deeds, we can open the Word to talk about the God of grace.

Christ came to earth to reveal God's grace to lost people. After He suffered and died to make eternal relationships with the Father possible, Jesus returned to heaven. But His primary objective—making God known—did not change: "Righteous Father, though the world does not know you, I know you, and they know that you have sent me. I have made you known to them, and *will continue to make you known* in order that the love you have for me may be in them and that I myself may be in them" (John 17:25-26, NIV, emphasis added).

Twice Jesus said His goal was to make God known. He said it once in the past tense and once in the future tense. Jesus *made* God known and *will continue to make* Him known. How could Jesus say this when He knew He would die the next day? How would He be able to *continue* to make God known? Through you and me. Through our deeds of mercy and words of truth, which are not really ours at all. They are part of Christ's ongoing self-revelation, signs of the kingdom that point people to the King.

So, don't forget to point to the Source of love! The receiver who catches a game-winning touchdown pass has the rapt attention of thousands. What does he do with it? Many athletes point heavenward, deflecting the crowd's praise to the One who made the hands that caught the ball and deserves praise for His wonderful design.[6] Merciful deeds attract attention too, particularly from those who haven't experienced much love and compassion in their lives. What do you do once you have their full attention? You deflect the praise by pointing them back to the Source.

Sometimes, however, even those of us who know the Lord forget to mention Him to those we serve. We can be so overwhelmed by worldly problems that we lose sight of heavenly things. All the hunger, poverty, oppression, abuse, and addiction—it can seem insurmountable. Our church has poured itself out into some very broken lives, and sometimes we've seen little fruit. We work our tails off, investing hours and dollars and tears. It's discouraging—especially when we are focused on earthly solutions and earthly outcomes. I'm ashamed to admit how often I have failed to pray for the people I serve. It reveals how much I depend on myself and the resources around me.

Hunger and poverty are God-ordained pathways into the lives of the people we are called to minister to. But if we limit our ministry to material assistance, our love is incomplete. And we aren't doing all that Jesus commanded us to do, as Oswald Chambers pointed out so well:

> Personal attachment to the Lord Jesus and to His perspective is the one thing that must not be overlooked. In missionary work the great danger is that God's call will be replaced by the needs of the people, to the point that human sympathy for those needs will absolutely overwhelm the meaning of being sent by Jesus. . . . We tend to forget that the one great reason underneath all missionary work is not primarily the elevation of the people, their education, nor their needs, but is first and foremost the command of Jesus Christ—"Go therefore and make disciples of all the nations."[7]

Jesus gave His church a "Great Commission" in Matthew 28:19. The first and foremost objective for God's people is to "make disciples," which means "to teach." We use words, especially, to communicate the *mind* of God and answer questions about Him. We perform deeds of mercy to communicate the *heart* of God. When it comes to teaching others about God, word and deed ministry are partners. A heart softened by mercy and compassion will be more open to the Word. As you share the Word, pray that it will impact the heart: "They said to each other, 'Did not our hearts burn within us while he talked to us on the road, while he opened to us the Scriptures?'" (Luke 24:32).

When delivered together, compassionate deeds and biblical words can affect both heart and mind. The combination can convince the skeptic and the sufferer that God exists and that He loves us.

SUMMARY

God uses His people to address physical needs—hunger, fear, injustice, and sickness. But we aren't being the church if we stop there. Human suffering results from a broken relationship with God. Our job isn't complete until we tell people about the God who loves to meet physical *and* spiritual needs.

Imagine how cold it is to live on the streets in the winter, to sleep on concrete, insulated only by layers of soggy newspaper. Now imagine slipping into a warm jacket handed to you by a kind stranger. Think of the soothing warmth that jacket brings to your wet, cold frame. God created the heat, He made the jacket, and He made us to be messengers who bring comfort and hope to those who are cold and suffering. We get to embody God's love to those who live in darkness and fear.

As we deliver deeds of mercy and love to others, we can tell them, "You think *I* care about you? Let me tell you about the One who *really* cares about you. He sent me here, and you can know Him too."

QUESTIONS FOR REFLECTION OR DISCUSSION

1. Do you find it easier to *tell* people about God's love, or to *show* it? Why?
2. Describe a time when you were spiritually hungry. What happened, and did God use other people in that experience?
3. Look around your community, workplace, and family. Pray that God would reveal places of fear and pain. How does God want you to respond?

CHAPTER 4

THE CREDIBILITY OF LOVE

Of all the needs (there are none imaginary) a lonely child has, the one that must be satisfied, if there is going to be hope and a hope of wholeness, is the unshaken need for an unshakable God.[1]

MAYA ANGELOU

Live such good lives among the pagans that, though they accuse you of doing wrong, they may see your good deeds and glorify God on the day he visits us.

1 PETER 2:12, NIV

Nine-year-old Emilia dragged her mother down six flights of stairs. Blood marked each step. The blow of a heavy pipe had cracked her mother's skull and paralyzed her body. Emilia was desperate to get her mother to the basement, safe from Emilia's uncle.

This wasn't Emilia's first brush with danger in the former Soviet republic where she lived. She was four when her father died. She had spent nights sleeping on the streets and in fields. Sometimes she foraged for food in trash cans. She avoided her mother's apartment, because drunk and violent men often came to visit. Her uncle was one of them, one of the men who would rape her and her mother, then steal what little they had.

This time, her mother's brother had come for more. As Emilia huddled in the basement with her mom, she wondered if he had found everything—the money they had scraped together, the train tickets to Russia, the clothes packed for their escape. Surely he had taken it all. It was the reason he broke in.

Terrified, penniless, and without anyone to help her, Emilia cared for her mother in the basement for three days, until she died.

A woman in their building enrolled Emilia in a state-run orphanage. It was a terrible place. Emilia escaped one day. They captured her quickly and brought her back. For several days she was beaten with chairs and pipes as punishment. Her painful bruises made it hard for her to sleep.

After her childhood of pain and abuse, Emilia endured nine more years of the same in the orphanage. "I felt I had no value," Emilia says. "No one showed me love. I believed that God had taken my parents away from me and had brought all this great suffering upon me. By the time I left the orphanage, I understood God to be very harsh and cruel."

In most countries, children have to leave orphanages when they turn eighteen. It's a very dangerous time in their young lives. Many of them (the majority of them, according to studies) will end up in jail or prostitution.[2]

When safety and love are foreign concepts to an eighteen-year-old orphan like Emilia, how do you persuade her that a loving God exists? To her, love was not only intangible, it was fiction. Before anyone could tell Emilia about the love of God, they had to make the idea of love itself concrete and credible.

That began at the House of Mercy, a ministry for girls leaving orphanages. In order to live there Emilia had to comply with rules and curfews like those at the orphanage. But there was a difference. Amid the structure Emilia also experienced gentleness: "I was angry, distrusting, and easily agitated, but I could tell I was in a good place."

Before long, a Christian family from the United States moved to town and reached out to Emilia: "They invited me to live in their home and help with chores. They used words I had never heard before: *excuse me* and *thank you*. I had always been treated like I was worthless. Joe and Maggie treated me like I was special, even lowering themselves to lift me up. They shared a table with me and gave me special dishes. They asked about my life. They included me in their family. These actions opened my heart to the Lord."

The deeds and words of kindness Emilia experienced were inexplicable to her. But they softened her heart to the truth about God's love. For the first time, the orphan felt it was possible to trust someone—her eternal Father. Today, Emilia is twenty-five years old and back at the House of Mercy as a staff member, pouring the love she received into the lives of young girls arriving from orphanages. She can tell them credibly about the love of God.

"Joe and Maggie's love and kindness were instrumental in me coming to the Lord," Emilia says. "They made me believe

I had worth." The God of all comfort showed Himself to Emilia and brought these verses to life: "Blessed be the God and Father of our Lord Jesus Christ, the Father of mercies and God of all comfort, who comforts [Emilia] in all [her] affliction, so that [she] may be able to comfort [other girls] who are in any affliction, with the comfort with which [she herself is] comforted by God" (2 Corinthians 1:3-4).

Did you notice what Joe and Maggie did for Emilia that made love tangible to her? It wasn't flashy or dramatic. They simply said *excuse me* and *thank you*. They were kind. They treated her with dignity and respect.

The first time I tasted baklava, I wanted more of the exotic delicacy. A lot more. It was that good. When Emilia tasted the unexpected sweetness of love, she wanted more. She was drawn to the Source[3] of love by the love she got from God's people. It started, though, with a taste test: "Oh, taste and see that the LORD is good! Blessed is the man who takes refuge in him!" (Psalm 34:8). The message of God's love becomes credible when we make God's love tangible through sacrificial service.

LOVE OPENS DOORS

Generosity surprises people. In a world that pursues the self-centered goals of wealth, comfort, and fame, altruism can get people's attention. The world is self-absorbed and expects everyone to be the same, so when believers adopt disabled children, tithe during a recession, and pour themselves out for others, people take notice.

Christ was the most other-centered person in history. We invite questions about Him when we live like Him. The apostle Peter faced persecution for his faith and wrote to others under persecution. In 1 Peter 3:13-17 he told his *persecuted* brothers and sisters to confidently prepare an explanation for their *hope*. Peter assumed they would be asked questions because something about their lives would attract attention.[4] So he encouraged them to have their *apologia*, or answer, ready to share. They should be prepared to "make a defense to anyone who asks you for a reason for the hope that is in you" (verse 15).

Is anyone asking about your hope? Are you ever asked why you live so differently from those around you? If no one is asking, perhaps you aren't doing enough to pique their curiosity. Christ calls us to be radically generous and other-centered.[5] When we are, people will see His work in our lives and be drawn to Him.

ALIEN ALTRUISM

When I tell people that my job involves helping widows and refugees and the poor, some of them respond, "Oh, that must be very rewarding!" I think this reveals a misunderstanding about the motivation for merciful deeds. Their response carries an implicit assumption that I must be in ministry because of the ways I benefit from it. Why else would I do something so challenging that pays so little? (I do, of course, like my work and it is frequently rewarding. But my income was the same eighteen years ago when I was a newspaper editor, and I work much harder now.)

If we do ministry because it is rewarding, we may burn out when it gets hard. Altruism is a different motivation for service—an "unselfish regard for or devotion to the welfare of others."[6] When believers live truly selfless lives we display an altruism that many in the secular world will find attractive, yet foreign. When we care for hurting people, let's be careful not to let them praise us for *our* altruism; instead, let's help them see that we possess an *alien altruism*.[7] Selfless deeds are a part of the apologetic of mercy because they reflect the ethics of another world—the kingdom of God.

Princeton University professor Robert George, author of *Making Men Moral: Civil Liberties and Public Morality*, argues that without God there is no credible reason to love your neighbor:

> Why . . . on a secularist understanding, should people restrain themselves—and even bear the sometimes-heavy burden of moral duties—out of regard for the rights of others? On purely atheistic and materialistic premises, how can it be rational for someone to bear heavy burdens and suffer great cost—perhaps even death—to honor other people's rights? No satisfactory answer is forthcoming. None, I submit, is possible.[8]

On the other side of the spectrum we find atheist Richard Dawkins. He thinks altruism is a defect, not a virtue. Dawkins believes that altruists within a species will soon be eliminated from the gene pool because selfishness is the key to survival. He wrote,

Even in the group of altruists, there will almost certainly be a dissenting minority who refuse to make any sacrifice. If there is just one selfish rebel, prepared to exploit the altruism of the rest, then he, by definition, is more likely than they are to survive and have children. Each of these children will tend to inherit his selfish traits. After several generations of natural selection, "the altruistic group" will be overrun by selfish individuals, and will be indistinguishable from the selfish group.[9]

According to Dawkins, survival depends on putting my needs first. Such thinking is the basis for the "me-first gospel" that could claim author and philosopher Ayn Rand as its chief prophet. She wrote,

Man—every man—is an end in himself, not a means to the ends of others; he must live for his own sake, neither sacrificing himself to others nor sacrificing others to himself; he must work for his *rational* self-interest, with the achievement of his own happiness as the highest moral purpose of his life.[10]

Dawkins and Rand argued that survival of the fittest and natural selection are the fundamental laws that guide human behavior. As such, it was hard for them to give a rational answer to the question, "Why is it good to care for the weak?"[11] After all, if the weak are coddled instead of culled, they will slow and weaken the herd, right?

When we abandon God as the Source of altruism and ultimate goodness, selfishness is what we have left. We can cover it up with good deeds so we appear less selfish, but our motivation is still selfishness!

Perhaps you don't like the word *selfish*. Instead, one could say that atheism leads people toward *autonomy* while Christ leads them toward *community*. Regardless, when "survival of the fittest" is the rule we follow, the only moral law is "every man for himself." Most people live according to that law, whether they acknowledge it or not. Believers offer the world a radical alternative.

Altruism is a powerful apologetic argument because it is so rare and unexpected. God's people serve others selflessly, not because we are inherently good, but because we resemble the selfless One who made us, saved us, and sent us to show His love to the world. He loved us, so we love the people He has made. Instead of Ayn Rand's "me-first gospel," Christians are motivated by Christ's "others-first" gospel:

Do nothing from selfish ambition or conceit, but in humility count others more significant than yourselves. Let each of you look not only to his own interests, but also to the interests of others. Have this mind among yourselves, which is yours in Christ Jesus, who, though he was in the form of God, did not count equality with God a thing to be grasped, but emptied himself, by taking the form of a servant, being born in the likeness of men. And being found in human form, he humbled himself by becoming

obedient to the point of death, even death on a cross.
(Philippians 2:3-8)

When we receive this other-centered Savior for ourselves, He begins a renovation project in our hearts that makes us more other-centered. Paul urged the church in Philippi to love one another *because of* the way Christ had loved them.

When you love others well, it should cause people to ask you, "What kind of person loves like this? Where could such sacrificial love come from?" When they ask, be ready to tell them the gospel, to point them back to Christ. When we do praiseworthy deeds of mercy, we must redirect that praise to God.

I know how tempting it is to accept praise for myself. I was an atheist from age eighteen to twenty-eight. I denied the existence of a good God, yet did many good deeds. (Many atheists do good deeds, of course. They just can't give a satisfying explanation as to why they *should*.[12]) In college I worked in soup kitchens and hosted Thanksgiving dinners in my fraternity house for two dozen orphans. I enjoyed it when others, especially girls, told me, "What a *nice* guy you are!"

Still, it bothered me to realize that praise from others was part of my motivation. So I resolved to keep my good deeds secret. It was surprisingly difficult to stay quiet about my soup kitchen visits. I did it, only to discover another layer of my self-centeredness. I felt *proud* of my *humility*. When I avoided the praise of others, I found self-praise flowing from my own proud heart.

I eventually surrendered my pride and asked Christ to rule my heart. That's when I discovered a new motive for good deeds—the gospel. I like this simple summary of the gospel message: *guilt*, *grace*, and *gratitude*. When I understood that claiming credit for my good deeds was sinful pride, I felt guilt. Then I learned of the grace that removed my guilt and gave me Christ's righteousness. Next I began to respond to grace with gratitude, serving others for the glory of my Savior and not myself.

GETTING OUT OF YOUR COMFORT ZONE

When I was an atheist, I wanted Christians to show me tangible proof of God's existence. Without proof, the Christian message lacked credibility.

While you and I can't provide nonbelievers with *proof* that God exists, we can provide *evidence*. Deeds of mercy are tangible evidence that what we believe about God is true. No one has to take a "blind leap of faith." We offer tangible love and then declare the intangible gospel so that people will see Christ. And then we trust the Holy Spirit, the only one who can persuade someone to believe, to give the gift of faith to the ones we serve.

So, here's my question: Are God's people providing evidence of His existence to the world? When the world looks at us, do they discover a radical love that makes Christianity credible?[13] Not often enough, I'm afraid. Christians are known for being *against* so many things these days. The world should know what we are *for*—peace and justice, the oppressed and downtrodden—as much as what we are against. We should be known for our servant position rather than our political position.

For this to happen, we have to get our hands dirty. We have to get uncomfortable. My friends and I often talk about the "Christian bubble" many of us live in. Deeply involved with people who look, talk, and think like we do, we rarely interact with the thousands of people around us. We hide "the light of the world" (see Matthew 5:14-16) under a basket of Christian community and church activities.

I remember seeing a megachurch with five baseball diamonds on the church property. They had a huge softball league of church members playing other church members. I wonder what opportunities for relational evangelism in their city they have missed.

I know you like to stay in your comfort zone. So do I. But, as long as God's people do that, we offer no comfort to those who need it. Jesus left His comfort zone, and so must we. According to the apostle John, "The Word became flesh and made his dwelling among us. We have seen his glory, the glory of the one and only Son, who came from the Father, full of grace and truth" (John 1:14, NIV). All of God's deeds of mercy in the Old Testament pointed forward to this ultimate act of mercy, the Incarnation. To redeem His people, the eternal Word of God had to become flesh. Jesus once lived in the most comfortable and exclusive neighborhood in the universe. Yet, He moved into the "slums"—*for you*. He is so other-centered that He left comfort behind, knowing pain and death were ahead. He was willing to do it for you.

Are you willing to go into the world and rub shoulders with those who don't know Jesus? God's people need to move proactively into people's lives (more on this in chapter 9). There are needy people all around the world, including your neighborhood and workplace. Their wounds cause them to doubt that God cares or even exists. Don't let fear or selfishness smother "the light of the world" that you carry everywhere you go. Love them, serve them, so that your alien altruism will grab their attention, make them ask questions, and open the doors of their hearts to Christ.

SUMMARY

To an orphan like Emilia, the Bible's claim that there is a loving Father in heaven who cares about orphans sounds rather incredible. *Un-credible*. But the tangible love of God's people gives us credibility when we say, "You do have a Father in heaven. He cares about you very much. That's why I'm here."

Mercy-minded Christians have a powerful opportunity to preach the gospel to hearts that have been softened by hardship. The merciful apologist labors in a crucial place, right on the boundary between human suffering and divine power. Francis and Edith Schaeffer lived on that boundary. Their sense of love for individuals was, as one long-term worker at L'Abri noted, "what made the difference."

What has been called their "pastoral touch" was not merely some professional skill they exercised as part of their paid ministry. . . . Love and truth went together, and truth was never to be an abstract intellectual concept. . . . [Schaeffer] knew that in a skeptical age influenced by relativism, Christian apologetics with its claim to absolute truth would not be taken seriously if Christians did not live out the truth.[14]

QUESTIONS FOR REFLECTION OR DISCUSSION

1. Do you hesitate to move into the lives of those around you? What holds you back?

2. How does practicing "alien altruism" look different from just helping others?

3. Blaise Pascal said we should "make good people wish that [Christianity] were true, and then show that it is."[15] How might you do that?

4. In 1 Peter 3:15, we are told to be "prepared to make a defense to anyone who asks you for a reason for the hope that is in you; yet do it with gentleness and respect." If Christianity is true, why does it matter how we communicate it? Does our presentation matter? Why or why not?

CHAPTER 5

THE CAUSE OF SUFFERING

Sin came into the world through one man, and death through sin, and so death spread to all men.

ROMANS 5:12

*The commanders of the army of the king of Assyria . . . captured Manasseh with hooks and bound him with chains of bronze and brought him to Babylon. And when he was in distress, he entreated the favor of the LORD his God and humbled himself greatly before the God of his fathers. He prayed to him, and God was moved by his entreaty and heard his plea and brought him again to Jerusalem into his kingdom. **Then Manasseh knew** that the LORD was God.*

2 CHRONICLES 33:11-13

There was a general in the Syrian army who was famous, powerful, and sick. He'd won many battles, achieved great things. But he had a disease that was slowly killing the nerves in his hands and feet. Despite his illness, he commanded the Syrian army shrewdly. His government honored him as a war hero and rewarded him generously for his victories.

A prisoner of war told the general that a cure for his illness existed in enemy-held territory. So the general procured an official letter demanding medical assistance. The letter would help, he thought. He was, however, asking his enemies for help. So he also brought along $4 million. Just in case. As the general and his staff left in search of the cure, his numb fingers clutched the bag of cash as tightly as they could.

The general, whose name was Naaman, had few concrete needs in his life—until he got leprosy. (You can read his story in 2 Kings 5.) That tangible need opened the door of Naaman's heart so that he could learn some intangible things about himself. God used the disease to reveal and humble Naaman's pride. God's intent was to heal Naaman's body and save his soul.

God's renovation of Naaman's life began with one of his own servants. She was an Israeli girl, a slave taken in battle. She told Naaman's wife about a prophet in Israel named Elisha who could heal him. Naaman's first lesson in humility was to listen to the most unlikely teacher of all, a young slave girl. She was a messenger of hope.

The general traveled to see Elisha. Still very self-reliant, Naaman brought the king's letter and lots of gold and silver to be sure he got what he came for. When Elisha sent a servant instead of speaking to the great general personally, Naaman's pride showed in his response: "Behold, I thought that he would surely come out to me and stand and call upon the name of the LORD his God, and wave his hand over the place and cure the leper" (2 Kings 5:11). Naaman was insulted that Elisha didn't come himself, and also that the prophet instructed him to bathe seven times in the muddy Jordan River.

A reluctant Naaman listened when his servants encouraged him to do what Elisha said. He humbled himself, took the plunge, and was healed. At that moment, the Lord restored not only Naaman's body, but also his soul. The physical healing led to knowledge of God in Naaman's heart and mind. "Then [Naaman] returned to [Elisha], he and all his company, and he came and stood before him. And he said, 'Behold, *I know* that there is no God in all the earth but in Israel. . . . From now on your servant will not offer burnt offering or sacrifice to any god but the LORD'" (2 Kings 5:15,17 emphasis added).

Without his leprosy, Naaman would never have listened to the slave girl, or traveled to Israel, or obeyed the servant's instructions to jump in the river. God used leprosy to expose Naaman's true problem—a proud, rebellious heart that needed cleansing. Naaman's heart was as numb as his hands.

As bad as his leprosy was, Naaman's sin problem was worse.[1] God's work in his life was complete, holistic, because it addressed Naaman's physical *and* spiritual needs. God could have (a) healed Naaman's disease and done nothing else, which would have left Naaman proud, comfortable, and spiritually dead, or (b) saved Naaman's soul and left him a leper. Many of God's children suffer with disease in this life.

Yet, God chose to heal Naaman both in body and soul. Illness and healing were the doorway into that particular man's heart. Naaman's leprosy kicked off a journey of internal and external healing. It's a great example of the apologetic of mercy at work.

My intent in this chapter is to help you be truly compassionate in your ministry, which requires you to understand the depth and origin of people's problems. (The good news only makes sense if we first understand the bad news.) In the last chapter I explained how deeds of mercy make God's love tangible and credible to hurting people. Chapters 6–10 will help you implement those ideas. But first, we must look at the underlying cause of pain.

WHY PEOPLE SUFFER

Sin is the root cause of all human suffering. This is the hard truth we all must face. I know it's not popular to talk about sin. It's not a great way to make friends.

Yet, anyone with eyes and ears must admit this world is a mess. Why is that? There must be *some* underlying cause for all the hatred, murder, theft, and deceit, right? Thomas Watson got it right when he said, "There'd never been a stone in the kidneys, if there had not been first a stone in the heart. Yea, the death of the body is the fruit and result of original sin."[2]

When a five-year-old child dies of leukemia, people often remark that it seems so wrong. Why should such a young one die? It just does not seem right. They are correct. It does not seem right because *it isn't right*. In the world God created before the Fall, there was no leukemia, or death, or tears. The image of God in each of us remembers this. We all know intuitively that such tragedies should not be. Ministry that combines word and deed is powerful because it offers a complete answer to a world in pain, as C. S. Lewis has said:

> Christianity is a fighting religion. It thinks God made the world — that space and time, heat and cold, and all the colours and tastes, and all the animals and vegetables, are things that God "made up out of His head" as a man makes up a story. But it also thinks that a great many things have gone wrong with the world that God made and that God insists, and insists very loudly, on putting them right again.[3]

Christianity alone offers a sufficient explanation — and solution — for the suffering in this world. Suffering is God's "megaphone to rouse a deaf world."[4] Pain is proof that something in the world just isn't right. God has told us that all human suffering is a result of a fractured relationship with Him.[5] If you think about it, there are only three causes of human suffering:

(1) My sin   (2) Another's sin   (3) Original sin

No matter what kind of suffering you encounter, the reason for it is one or more of those three kinds of sin. If I get drunk and smash my car into yours, all three causes of suffering are at work. In my sin I drink too much and cause an accident. Your car is damaged because of my sin. And original sin is the reason people get drunk in the first place. I have described this to secular social workers, and while they would rather refer to sin as "mistakes" or "poor choices," they at least recognize that their clients are afflicted by their own sin and the sins of others.

Recognizing sin is one thing. Removing it is quite another. While secular social workers may admit that sin has caused a client's suffering, what can they do about it? They may address the symptoms, but what about the underlying wound? What about hope for permanent relief? If our only hope is in food stamps and rent assistance, the ache in our souls will never be healed.

We suffer because we are separated from God. Reunion with Him is the only lasting cure for our pain. In truth, the gospel is God's solution to *eternal* suffering.[6] I am not saying the gospel has no earthly impact. What I mean is that God created the church as His instrument both to bring people *into* eternal relationship with Him and to address earthly suffering caused *by* that broken relationship. God changes His people internally and eternally before sending us out to change the world.

When God's people are doing true gospel ministry, they do not neglect humankind's true problem—broken fellowship with God caused by sin. Even when we serve those victimized by the sins of other people, we cannot forget that victims also need Christ's forgiveness for their own sins.

God has often used physical brokenness to help people see their spiritual brokenness. Psalm 107:17-22 says God punishes sinful people in order to elicit cries of repentance from them so that He can heal and deliver them. (These very good things are only made possible because the people were afflicted enough to repent!) David and Paul wrote about the blessings of affliction that lead us to God: "It is good for me that I was afflicted, that I might learn your statutes" (Psalm 119:71). "Indeed, we felt that we had received the sentence of death. But that was to make us rely not on ourselves but on God who raises the dead" (2 Corinthians 1:9).

My friend James Mullings is doing incarnational ministry in southeast Washington, DC. He bought a home one hundred yards from one of the country's most dangerous high schools so that he could build relationships with the young people there, provide tutoring in his basement, and share the gospel with them. James has seen many effects of the Fall in that community. He told me, "I think God uses suffering because no one wants to admit their sinfulness. So He uses suffering as a manifestation of the brokenness of our souls. God puts physical brokenness in our lives in order to reveal to us our spiritual poverty."

James' ministry is effective because it is holistic—he ministers to both the spiritual and physical needs of the teens in his neighborhood. He loves them in word and deed, knowing they suffer from both spiritual and physical brokenness. James is following the example of Jesus.[7]

When Jesus healed broken human bodies, He also dealt with the brokenness hidden inside. In Mark 2, a paralyzed man was brought by his friends to Jesus to be healed. Before Jesus healed the man's body, He healed the man's soul and forgave his sins. Jesus addressed the man's sin problem first, because sin is the root cause of all suffering.[8] Then, Jesus addressed the consequences of human sin by healing the man. Jesus provided complete healing that recognized the man's dual nature. It was a comprehensive kingdom experience—word and deed for body and soul.

Our deeds of mercy are like an injection of hope for hurting hearts. But we must offer hope for eternal, rather than temporary, healing.

THE BAD NEWS MAKES THE GOOD NEWS GOOD

Earthly suffering is not the fundamental problem the gospel addresses. That's where the Social Gospel went wrong, making deed ministry the very definition of gospel ministry.

The gospel is always described in radical terms. It is about darkness and light, people resurrected from spiritual death to eternal life. This radical cure indicates we have a radical illness. Sin is our true problem, so we must talk about it if we intend to proclaim the gospel of Jesus Christ. The bad news about our sin is what makes the good news mean something.

People need to be called to repent of sin because their eternal destiny is at stake. Think about it this way: The college roommate you choose is less important than the spouse you choose. You'll live with a roommate for a year or two. You will spend decades with your spouse. Deeds of mercy bless people for a short time on earth.[9] Words of truth can bless people for eternity.

I challenge you to name a food program, orphanage, or medical mission that offers something better than eternal life. What "good news" is better than that? Don't get me wrong—good deeds are important and urgently needed. But good deeds are a by-product of the good news and should point back to it.

Many people refuse the Savior because they don't think they need saving. They can accept deeds of mercy from God's people. They can believe Jesus was a prophet who said some interesting things. But to call Jesus Savior implies that they are lost and sinful. They think, *I'm not that bad, and God's not that mad.* Popular false teachers have misled millions about their spiritual poverty, downplaying the problem of sin or denying it outright.

Robert Schuller's Crystal Cathedral was, appropriately enough, two miles south of Disneyland. In Schuller's fantasy-land version of Christianity, our problem isn't sin. Our problem is self-esteem. Human beings love to hear that, to be told they are great and can solve their own problems. It's no wonder Schuller's books have been best sellers, with titles such as *Way to the Good Life, Move Ahead with Possibility Thinking, Self-Love, Self-Esteem: The New Reformation,* and *Living Positively One Day at a Time.*

Schuller has not only avoided talking about sin, but in a 1985 interview with *Time* Schuller actually said it is *wrong* to do so:

I don't think anything has been done in the name of Christ and under the banner of Christianity that has proven more destructive to human personality and, hence, counter-productive to the evangelism enterprise, than the often crude, uncouth, and unchristian strategy of attempting to make people aware of their lost and sinful condition.[10]

My intent here isn't to beat up on Robert Schuller. The problem is in our own hearts. Preachers like him make fortunes because people with "itching ears" would rather hear myths that make them feel good about themselves than the truth (see 2 Timothy 4:3-4). The popular message of self-esteem and self-love claims that my salvation lies within myself—that I just need to realize how great I really am! By contrast, the gospel of Jesus Christ tells me that salvation cannot come from myself, because *I am the problem*! That message doesn't sell as many books, but it's true.

Let me be clear. The good news about Jesus isn't good without the bad news about sin. You may feel I am belaboring this point. But I'm almost done, and this is important because so many Christians have neglected souls in their commitment to serving bodies. Our good deeds have no lasting goodness unless we tell people the cause of their suffering and that they are sinners who need a Savior (see Mark 1:14-15). That is the gospel—the best news of all. Perhaps you've heard the illustration of a woman relaxing in the pool when a lifeguard shouts, "Good news! I'm here to save you!" He dives in, and she stares at him like he's crazy. His "rescue" seems ridiculous, because she's not in danger. The next day, her child falls into the deep end and begins to drown. The boy is going underwater for the second time when the lifeguard shouts, "Good news! I'm here to save you!" He dives in and rescues the boy, and the woman thanks him profusely.

The lifeguard said and did the same thing both times. What made the difference? When her son was drowning, the boy desperately needed a rescuer, so the lifeguard's words and deeds were truly good news to the mother and her son.

Similarly, for us to believe the good news, we must recognize the danger. We must understand the bad news — that we are sinners who must repent. When we do, when we bow the knee and acknowledge our need, then Christ and all His sufficiency can come streaming into our hearts as good news.

If your primary goal is to make people like you — or even to make them like Christ — then you may hesitate to say things they won't like. You may focus on deed ministry and avoid spiritual discussions. I know that calling people to repentance won't make you popular, and it isn't easy. But it is not optional. Jesus said that "repentance and forgiveness of sins should be proclaimed in his name to all nations" (Luke 24:47). Our job is to share the full gospel and leave the results to God.

The gospel message we proclaim will elicit one of two responses:

> But thanks be to God, who in Christ always leads us in triumphal procession, and through us spreads the fragrance of the knowledge of him everywhere. For we are the aroma of Christ to God among those who are being saved and among those who are perishing, to one a fragrance from death to death, to the other a fragrance from life to life. (2 Corinthians 2:14-16)

When they hear the gospel, people who know they are lost will come running into the arms of the Savior. Those who refuse to see their sin will be infuriated by the call to repentance. The true gospel will make some people uncomfortable, even angry, because it tells them bad news about themselves. Some people will reject the gospel, and Christ, and you. Remember it is really God they reject, just as people have for centuries. If you clearly, lovingly, and humbly proclaim the gospel, then you can have peace and leave the results to God.

SUMMARY

Pain and suffering are a daily reality for millions of people. The body of Christ is called to do what we can to alleviate physical suffering. If we want to do any lasting good, however, we must help people see that they have spiritual needs more profound than any of their physical needs.

The problems we encounter in life are consequences of sin. Faith in Christ is the only thing that can address the disease (sin), but Christ's people can address the symptoms (physical suffering). When we do, we provide tangible evidence that God is at work in the world and truly cares about every level of human need.

QUESTIONS FOR REFLECTION OR DISCUSSION

1. Why is it often hard to tell people about their need to repent? How can we make that conversation easier?
2. From your own experience, what are some examples of treating the symptoms of sin instead of dealing with the heart of sin?
3. How could you begin spiritual conversations with people you are helping in material ways?
4. What role does your own repentance play in calling others to repent?

THE APOLOGETIC OF MERCY: *HOW*

To be a witness does not consist in engaging in propaganda nor even in stirring people up, but in being a living mystery. It means to live in such a way that one's life would not make sense if God did not exist.[1]

Emmanuel Suhard

Jesus said to them again, "Peace be with you. As the Father has sent me, even so I am sending you."

John 20:21

CHAPTER 6

NAMES

God is all this to you: if you hunger He is bread to you; if you thirst He is water to you; if you are in darkness, He is light to you.[1]

AUGUSTINE

*But the L*ORD *is a refuge to his people, a stronghold to the people of Israel. So you shall know that I am the L*ORD *your God.*

JOEL 3:16-17

One of the darkest places God's people are working today is the world of human trafficking and slavery. There are more slaves today than at any point in history.[2] Yet, God is using International Justice Mission (IJM) to do incredible things. In the Philippines, Thailand, India, and other nations, God's people at IJM "proclaim liberty to the captives" and have freed thousands of them. When they do, they make the mercy and love of God tangible. They help people see God.

Marian is a young woman in the Philippines. She left her school and home to get away from her parents, who were strung out on drugs. Tragically, Marian fell into the same trap as millions of other young people on the streets.

A friend told Marian she could get free room and board in Cebu City. All she had to do was dance in a bar. Marian quickly learned that the men in the bar would be doing more than watching her dance. "After they used us," said Marian, "the customers would just go to sleep." Marian had become one of millions of enslaved women and children around the world.

IJM staff in the Philippines helped rescue Marian and nineteen other captives after one of the girls escaped and reported what was happening at the bar. Fourteen of them were minors. Marian and the others entered aftercare programs and homes where they began to heal. Through God's grace, Marian eventually enrolled in college and is now a mentor to other victims.

Her transformation from slave to mentor began when God sent His people into dark places to do His work. And Marian sees that it was God who sent them. She says, "Most of all I thank God because *now I see that He loves me — because He sent you to rescue me.*" For Marian, God isn't a distant idea or philosophy. He isn't abstract. In concrete ways, Marian discovered that she could call God her Rescuer.[3]

WHAT'S IN A NAME?

I once took a list of about four hundred names and descriptions of God in the Bible and divided them into two columns. One column described who God *is* and the other what God *does*. In the "who God is" column I put: Holy One, Lord, Mighty God, and Sovereign Lord. When I finished, I had about two hundred of these powerful, imposing, and majestic descriptions.[4] But they didn't move me as much as the ones in the second column, where I put names and descriptions referring to God's actions in our lives. Some of my favorites from the two hundred on that list are:

- Abba (Father) — Romans 8:14-17
- Comforter — John 14:16,26
- Defender of Orphans — Psalm 10:14
- Deliverer — Romans 11:26
- Father of Mercies — 2 Corinthians 1:3
- Father to His Children — Psalm 103:13-14,17-18
- God My Savior — Luke 1:47
- God Who Sees Me — Genesis 16:13
- Guarantee — Ephesians 1:14
- Hiding Place — Psalm 32:7
- Intercessor — Hebrews 7:25
- Light That Leads to Life — John 8:12
- The Lord My Fortress — Psalm 18:2
- The Lord Who Provides — Genesis 22:14
- Loving Ally — Psalm 144:2
- Our Advocate — Hebrews 9:24; 1 John 2:1-2
- Our Peace — Ephesians 2:14
- Redeemer — Isaiah 59:20; Job 19:25-26
- Refuge — Psalm 61:3
- Savior in Times of Trouble — Jeremiah 14:8

- Shelter—Isaiah 25:4
- Strength and Song—Isaiah 12:2
- Strong Fortress—Psalm 31:2
- Unfailing Love—Psalm 59:10

These descriptions of God tell us *what He does for us.* God tailors His ministry to each of our needs, and He even uses you and me to carry out His ministry—perhaps in the way a doctor prescribes medication but a pharmacist dispenses it (see 1 Corinthians 3:6-7).

The rest of this book is about how God can use you to reveal Himself in the tangible ways described by His names. The God who says, "I am he who comforts you" (Isaiah 51:12) often uses the body of Christ to provide His comfort. Paul made that clear when he described God as "the Father of mercies and God of all comfort, who comforts us in all our affliction, *so that we* may be able to comfort those who are in any affliction, with the comfort with which we ourselves are comforted by God" (2 Corinthians 1:3-4, emphasis added).

One week after Hurricane Katrina, I flew to Biloxi, Mississippi, with two buddies. We spent a week patching damaged roofs, and two years later I went with a larger team to do complete roof replacements. We always encouraged people to see God as their Shelter and Refuge. After all, we were there on His behalf, helping to provide them with shelter and refuge. Marian in the Philippines saw God as Redeemer, Comforter, and Savior after His people came to redeem, comfort, and save her. When Jesus uses your hands to distribute food to a hungry family, you help them see God as the Lord Who Provides. When you stand with a persecuted refugee in court, she discovers that God is a Loving Ally and Advocate. As we saw in chapter 4, God used Naaman's need for healing to reveal Himself as Jehovah-Raphah — I Am Your Healer.

THE NAME *YAHWEH*

God often combines His name Jehovah in that way, to help us know Him. Jehovah, or *Yahweh*, means "I Am." This unusual name appears about seven thousand times[5] in the Old Testament, but is more of a statement than a description. Why did God choose to use this mysterious name more than any other? Let's look at the day Moses first learned to call God *I Am*:

> Then Moses said to God, "If I come to the people of Israel and say to them, 'The God of your fathers has sent me to you,' and they ask me, 'What is his name?' what shall I say to them?" God said to Moses, "I AM WHO I AM." And he said, "Say this to the people of Israel, 'I AM has sent me to you.'"
> (Exodus 3:13-14)

When God told Moses His name is *I Am*, Moses was getting ready to lead the children of Israel out of Egypt, where they were enslaved. Who was the only One who could free them? "I Am," said the Lord. Still, Moses knew the people were going to ask him for further explanation, because even the longer version of the name, "I Am Who I Am," is a mystery. Knowing that the people, given all they had suffered, would find it hard to believe the promised rescue was real, God shared more about His name: "Say this to the people of Israel, '[I Am], the God of your fathers, the God of Abraham, of Isaac, and the God of Jacob, has sent me to you.' This is my name forever, and thus I am to be remembered throughout all generations" (verse 15).

God wanted the slaves in Egypt to know that although they'd been there for four hundred years, He had not forgotten them. He had been with them the entire time. The God of their ancestors was still their God. It's as if He was saying, "I Am, and have always been, your God. So trust Me." He told the people that the incomprehensible and infinite Creator whom their ancestors worshipped would become comprehensible through a dramatic rescue mission. God's presence would make Him known to them in tangible ways. He remained transcendent and radically *other*, yet God was *with* Moses and the people because they needed Him: "I have surely seen the affliction of my people who are in Egypt and have heard their cry because of their taskmasters. I know their sufferings, and I have come down to deliver them out of the hand of the Egyptians" (verses 7-8).

Why did God come to rescue these people? Did they deserve His help? Was it because in the midst of foreign gods they remained faithful to the God of Abraham, Isaac, and Jacob? Or because they were more attractive, more dutiful, more deserving of rescue than slaves in other countries? No. The Exodus was not a reward to the Israelites for anything they did. God came down to rescue them because (a) they needed help, and (b) He is the Helper.

The Exodus revealed who God is. The name He revealed to Moses, I Am, is an invitation to all people who need help. (Like you. Like me.) It is an unfinished sentence that becomes complete when we see God through the lens of our need. In their book *We Would See Jesus*, Roy and Revel Hession explain this powerfully. Don't miss this:

> "I am" is an unfinished sentence. It has no object. I am — what? Great is our wonder when we discover, as we continue with our Bibles, that He is saying, "I AM whatever My people need," and that the sentence is purposely left blank so that man may bring his many and various needs, as they arise, to complete it!
>
> Apart from human need, this great name of God goes round and round in a closed circle, "I am that I am" — which means that God is incomprehensible. But the moment human need and misery present themselves, He becomes just what that person needs. . . . Do we lack peace? "I am thy peace," says He. Do we lack strength? "I am thy strength." Do we lack spiritual life? "I am thy life." . . .
>
> Every now and then we come across "Jehovah" compounded with another word to form His completed name for that occasion. . . . "Jehovah-Nissi" . . . means "I am thy banner" (Exodus 17:15). "Jehovah-Shalom" [means] "I am thy peace" (Judges 6:24). . . . "Jehovah-Tsidkenu" [means] "I am thy righteousness" (Jeremiah 23:6). . . . So it goes on, seven such wonderful compounds of Jehovah, seven

places in the Old Testament, where the check "I am" is filled in for us for our encouragement.[6]

Each time a new need arises in our lives, it is a new opportunity for us to learn something about our Father in heaven and His ability to provide for us. I like to put it this way: *Adversity is our opportunity to learn God's sufficiency.*

THE NAME *JESUS*

The name *I Am* is all over the Old Testament. In the New Testament, the name Jesus takes center stage. This name reveals even more about how God provides for the needs of His people.

The name *Jesus* actually appears in the Old Testament too. Joshua's name in Hebrew is *Yehoshua*. In the gospel of Matthew we find a later form of the same name, *Yeshua*. Matthew goes on to tell us that the name *Yeshua* was not picked by Joseph, but by Jesus' heavenly Father, who told Joseph, "You shall call his name Jesus, for he will save his people from their sins" (Matthew 1:21). The little word *for* is usually significant in Scripture. Read it as *because*, and the meaning of the name Jesus becomes clear.

Of course, the Father could have given His Son any name. Why recycle *Yeshua* (Joshua) from the Old Testament, particularly for the most unique baby every born? Consider that Joshua's name at birth was actually *Hoshea*, meaning *salvation* or *savior*. It's a fitting name because Joshua was the man who would lead Israel from the desert into the Promised Land.[7]

Later, God changed Hoshea's name, adding the prefix *Yeho* (from God's name *Yahweh*) to make the name Joshua. The new name meant "*Yahweh* is salvation." God chose the name Joshua to make sure He received the glory for all that Joshua did.

Jesus' ministry repeats and perfects Joshua's ministry. God used Joshua to shepherd His people and bring them to the Promised Land. Jesus came to shepherd His people and bring them to heaven. So He is given the same name as Joshua. But Jesus went further. He did something Joshua never did: Jesus claimed the covenant name I Am for Himself (see John 8:58; 18:6). Jesus, whose name means "*Yahweh* is salvation," explicitly said, "*I Am" the Messiah,* your salvation (see 4:26).

This is the purpose of the Incarnation: divine rescue of God's people through a person named *Yahweh* Saves. Why spend so much time talking about the meaning of Jesus' name? Because if you are part of His body and do ministry in His name, you need to know what His ministry is all about.

Jesus didn't come to make people more comfortable, to serve our felt needs alone. He healed and fed many people, then He returned to heaven, leaving many more sick and hungry people behind. Nor did Jesus come merely to answer our questions. His name is not *Yahweh Teaches*. His name is "I am your salvation" because Jesus came to earth on a rescue mission focused neither on our bodies nor our minds alone. He came to rescue our souls.

So, when you tell people about Jesus, consider whether you are describing Him as merely an answer for their bodily needs or their intellectual skepticism. You don't want them to hope in better circumstances or better understanding. The only source of real hope, of *a living hope*, is the resurrection of Jesus: "According to his great mercy, he has caused us to be born again to a living hope through the resurrection of Jesus Christ from the dead" (1 Peter 1:3). Cornelius Plantinga, former president of Calvin Theological Seminary, has said,

> Preaching, sacraments, evangelism, and Christian social action . . . all center on the resurrection of Jesus Christ. To the desperate and bewildered, Christians say, "The Lord is risen." To doubters, Christians say, "The Lord is risen." To martyrs who sing to God while their enemies set them on fire, Christians say, "The Lord is risen." To poor people in Bangladesh, or Honduras, or Turkey, who suffer first the indignity of their poverty and then the desolation of being blown out of their houses by hurricanes or washed out by flood — to these people Christians say, "The Lord is risen." Proclamation of the resurrection of Jesus isn't nearly everything Christians have to offer the world, but it's the platform for everything they have to offer. Every Christian hospital, college, orphanage, media ministry, counseling service . . . builds on this platform.[8]

SUMMARY

When we combine deeds of mercy with words of truth, we take apologetics out of the classroom and into the streets.

There, we have the privilege of introducing the suffering to their Comforter. We intercede for those held captive by sin, drugs, alcohol, and slavery and tell them about their Redeemer and Rescuer.

People who suffer in tangible ways long for God's help in tangible ways. Martin Luther discovered the presence of God when he wrote "A Mighty Fortress Is Our God." At that time in his life, Luther really needed a fortress. Condemned as a heretic by Emperor Charles V and the Catholic Church, Luther had to run for his life. He took secret shelter in Wartburg Castle, where he worked on a German translation of the Bible and wrote,

> A mighty fortress is our God, a bulwark never failing;
> Our helper He, amid the flood of mortal ills prevailing. . . .
> And though this world, with devils filled, should
>   threaten to undo us,
> We will not fear, for God hath willed His truth to
>   triumph through us.

Luther had known Jesus for years. He had written marvelous things about God and His character. But Luther had more to learn. In that castle he experienced the "pragmatic presence of God."[9] Luther learned that God was truly a strong fortress, a shield of protection and a tower of safety—because that was what he needed from God at that time. It wasn't head knowledge for Luther, but heart knowledge, perceived only when his great need allowed him to see God in new ways.

QUESTIONS FOR REFLECTION OR DISCUSSION

1. Does a particular title or description of God on pages 75–76 mean something special to you? How has a need in your life helped you see God in new ways?

2. Are you aware of the needs of those around you? What could your neighbors or friends learn about God through your deeds of kindness? What name or title of God could you help them experience for themselves?

3. How can you point people to Christ as you serve them, so they see that He is the Source of their help?

CHAPTER 7

PRESENCE

The Word became flesh and dwelt among us.

JOHN 1:14

I will lay sinews upon you, and will cause flesh to come upon you, and cover you with skin, and put breath in you, and you shall live, and you shall know that I am the LORD.

EZEKIEL 37:6

The LORD *is near to the brokenhearted and saves the crushed in spirit.*

PSALM 34:18

It was over 100 degrees in the dark garage. The family had no food or water. But they spent all day and night inside, because outside were killers with machetes. Fabris Vuninka and his family were hiding from Hutus who were hunting Tutsis. The genocide in Rwanda had spilled over into Congo. Members of Fabris's family were kidnapped and never seen again. Others were killed outright, including Fabris's father.

The family survived that night, and soon the Red Cross took them to a refugee camp in Benin. In late February 2000, Catholic Charities helped them settle in Richmond, Virginia, in a neighborhood with several thousand other refugees. This community, called Nottingham Green, is right next to West End Presbyterian Church. It wasn't long before Fabris met volunteers from West End who put on an "X Games" for children from the neighborhood.

Volunteers would sometimes tell Fabris, "God loves you!" Fabris would think, *I don't think so*. Where was the love of God in all that had happened to him? "I thought about my life and I wondered, how can they say He loves me?"

Fabris wasn't the first to ask that question. We can tell people all day long, "Jesus loves you." Many will reply as Fabris did: "I don't think so." The existence of evil, particularly evil that has affected them personally, causes them to doubt. I'm sure you have heard people say, "If your God is so good and powerful, why are there all these problems in the world?" Or, "I can't believe in a God who would allow suffering."

These questions are so common that an entire branch of apologetics exists to provide answers for them. Such an answer is called a theodicy. (See the Resources section for a list of good books on this topic.) But you don't have to know that word, or what it means. *Your presence* is a powerful response to people's doubts. People who doubt that God even exists can experience His tangible love through the compassionate presence of His people.

That presence is what grabbed the attention of Fabris. "The

first three hours of Saturday are the time when everyone wants to be in bed, but these people from the church were out there smiling and running around like they were so thrilled to be awake and playing with us. I asked some of them why they did this. They said God was the reason, but I didn't understand. I was so blind. I didn't see that Jesus was all over that place."

Fabris was impressed by the West End volunteers and their deeds of mercy, deeds that made their words of truth credible. After games and snacks, the gospel was explained at every X Games event. Dozens of refugee children heard who Jesus is and what a relationship with Him means.

The things Fabris heard about Jesus intrigued him. He wanted to know more. Soon he was attending the youth group at West End. There he confessed a desire to believe in Jesus, although he didn't know how. He and his youth leader prayed together for nearly a year, until one day it just clicked. Jesus Christ, the X in West End's X Games, moved into Fabris's heart and began remaking him from within. Jesus revealed Himself to Fabris—first through the deeds of church volunteers, then through the Word of God and the work of the Holy Spirit in his heart.

Now twenty-five, Fabris works three jobs and is paying his own way through his last year of college. He hopes to go back to Congo and start programs to serve children there. Until then, God is keeping him busy here. In the past three years Fabris has taught twenty refugees from Nottingham Green how to drive. They all drive his car, which has the license plate *JlovesNG*—"Jesus loves Nottingham Green."

Fabris says, "We use my own vehicle, my gas. They don't pay me a penny. But they all ask *why*. Why I do it? I tell them it is because of what Jesus has done for me." Fabris has taught atheists, Jews, Muslims, Hindus, and Buddhists to drive. "They tell their friends about me, but they don't just say that I'm a nice guy. They understand there is something about me that *makes* me a nice person. They usually avoid saying Jesus' name, but they know that He is the reason I do this."

Fabris now replicates the incarnational ministry he experienced. His own story of pain and hardship combines with his deeds of mercy to make him a credible and effective witness. That's what chapters 7 and 8 are about: how Jesus ministers to us personally and then uses us to do His ministry, through our *proactive presence.* In this chapter we will look at what it means to be *present.* In the next chapter we will consider how to be *proactive* in our ministry to others.

JESUS' LOVING PRESENCE IN THE WORLD

On the night before He died, Jesus said, "Truly, truly, I say to you, whoever believes in me will also do the works that I do; and greater works than these will he do, because I am going to the Father" (John 14:12). How can believers in Christ do *even greater* things than Jesus did? The Greek word for "greater" is also used in Scripture to communicate the ideas "more" and "abundant." Jesus wasn't saying our ministry would be of greater *value* than His ministry. He was referring to the scope and extent of what He would do through us. Once His physical body left the earth, Jesus delegated His ministry to the body of Christ. This body — the church — quickly grew to include thousands and then millions of men and women and children.

Today, His Word is available in nearly three thousand languages, and there are over four hundred thousand missionaries around the world.[1] Christ is doing more abundant work today, more widespread work, through His many brothers and sisters. The body of Christ is Jesus' loving presence in every part of the world.

Mother Teresa understood this. The world saw a love in her that grabbed their attention, but she didn't want people to focus on her. She always pointed to Christ as the Source of her love: "Jesus went about doing good. And we are trying to imitate him now because I believe that God loves the world through us. Just as he sent Jesus to be his love, his presence in the world, so today he is sending us."[2]

Whether God has placed you in the streets of Calcutta or the suburbs of Charlotte, you have opportunities to be His compassionate presence, to make His love tangible to hurting people.

What does *tangible love* look like? Think of it as *incarnate words*. If I merely tell a lonely widow, "Jesus loves you!" and "God is good!" my words are as two-dimensional as a bumper sticker. God's love isn't tangible until that lonely woman actually *sees* and *feels* love. There is a big difference between love as an idea and love in action.

If you are in a dark basement, the idea of light is no help at all. You need a flashlight. If your children are hungry, the idea that God cares won't fill their bellies. Your family needs food. When God's people provide food, hold your hand, pray with you, and give you hope, they can declare, "Jesus loves you!" with authenticity. But it requires the investment of our time, talent, and emotion. It requires our compassionate presence.

PEOPLE OR PAPERWORK?

Remember those folks from Hotel Employees International Union Local 25? Well, soon after Jorge distributed the cards and Bibles we had given him, he heard from other organizations that wanted to provide assistance to the laid-off workers. They offered financial help, but did not offer their presence.

One large religious charity asked the Local 25 office to do all the face-to-face work for them. They instructed the union staff to interview members with needs, complete an application for assistance, and then fax the paperwork to the charity's office. Then the charity staff paid the utility bills, mortgages, and such directly—without any interaction with the union members. Effectively, this ministry that claimed to represent Christ did their work in a way that looked very little like Christ's ministry. By never meeting with the people they helped, they treated the union members like bills to be paid, rather than real people with emotional and spiritual needs.

We resolved to do something more personal. We invited sixty members of Local 25 to come to our church on two different nights to receive assistance. Knowing in advance the ethnicity and first language of each guest, we tried to pair them with appropriate counselors. We recruited Korean, Ethiopian, and

Latino elders, deacons, pastors, and church members to be counselors and friends that night.

One of the counselors was an Ethiopian pastor. I had called him to say we needed a counselor who spoke Amharic to communicate with an Eritrean man from the union. "Uh, do you know anything about the problems between Ethiopia and Eritrea?" the pastor asked. "No," I said, "but if you both speak Amharic that's what matters." "You don't understand," he replied. "Our countries have been at war for a long time. We *really* don't get along." I naively assured him it would be fine. I was just eager to have a Christian counselor who spoke the right language.

When the union members arrived at the church they were introduced to their counselors for the evening. Together, they got a cup of coffee and a snack. They stood and chatted before entering the fellowship hall. There we had twenty small tables where the counselors began forming friendships with the guests. They discussed how things had been since 9/11. The counselors asked about their health, their children, their concerns. We encouraged the counselors to focus on building relationships and sharing from Scripture, rather than merely discussing finances. Most of the guests heard the gospel explained by their counselor.

Before any of that, though, the Ethiopian pastor had something to say to his Eritrean guest: "My friend, I need to ask your forgiveness for what my country has done to your people." The other man replied, "No, I am the one who must ask *you* for forgiveness on behalf of my country." They stared at one another for a moment, and then they both smiled. Having given and received forgiveness from one another, the men prayed together. Then they discussed that union member's needs.

The counselors spent thirty to forty minutes in conversation with their guests. Then they brought their bills to a desk where two deacons were writing checks. Together with the counselors, the deacons made decisions about which bills to pay. Each counselor was also given a copy of the *Jesus* film[3] and a Bible in the guest's first language. The counselors returned to their guests with these items and the checks, where they explained everything was an expression of God's love and compassion. Then they prayed together.

I don't claim that this is a perfect example of compassionate presence or incarnational ministry. Few long-term relationships were built that night (that is the best way to have a lasting impact in someone's life). I share this story to show the contrast between this approach and one that simply treats people as paperwork to be processed. Human beings are not administrative tasks we must deal with, and the church is not a bill-paying service!

GIVE YOURSELF

As the phrase "pour yourself out" (Isaiah 58:10) implies, it takes effort to do the kind of ministry God calls us to. It actually takes something more precious than effort: *time.* In the busy world we live in, time is often our most treasured commodity. Giving your time and presence to people communicates love in a way words cannot.

At our church, we often need to purchase food, clothing, or other items for the people we serve. It would be convenient to simply give them gift cards to Target or the grocery store, but that would waste a great opportunity to give them our presence.

Instead, we go shopping with them. Our deacons and mercy committee understand that ministry is about more than getting the shoes or the school supplies. Those material needs simply open doors into relationship. The shopping, the time in the car, the cup of coffee or lunch afterward—all are opportunities to be present with the people we help. The benefits are not always *measurable*, but they certainly are *tangible*.

Another example: In 2008 my wife had her first cancer surgery. She was in the operating room for five hours. Tom Holliday, our pastor, sat in the waiting room with me the entire time. In order to be there with me, Tom had to cancel some counseling appointments and delay his sermon preparation. He sacrificed to give me the gift of his presence. It made a huge difference. I had tangible evidence that Tom (and God through Tom's presence) cared for us.

THE PRESENCE OF CHRIST

There was another person there with me in that waiting room, a person who didn't have to reschedule appointments to be there. Jesus was with me—the one person who would never leave my side. One of the most powerful things we can tell people about Christ is that when you believe in Him, when you ask Him to be Lord of your life, He will be with you in every circumstance—good and bad.

Pastor Lon Solomon and his wife experienced this at a hospital one night. It was 2:30 a.m. They stood alone outside the emergency room while a half dozen doctors and nurses worked on their unconscious young daughter. Without any friends or family present with them, it was a time anyone might have felt "cosmic loneliness." But Solomon says they did not feel alone:

> Because standing there next to me in that emergency room, I didn't have Islam with all of its rules; I didn't have Judaism with all of its empty rituals; or Buddhism with all of its enlightenment. Standing next to me there in that emergency room, I had the living, risen Christ, who had His arm around me, whispering in my ear, "Lon, don't worry about it. I'm here, and it's going to be okay."
>
> When the storms of life hit us, and they do, we can find comfort in knowing that we aren't alone. Jesus said:

> I will never leave you nor forsake you. (Hebrews 13:5)

> Behold, I am with you always, to the end of the age. (Matthew 28:20)

> When you pass through the waters, I will be with you; and through the rivers, they shall not overwhelm you; when you walk through fire you shall not be burned, and the flame shall not consume you. (Isaiah 43:2)

Solomon continues, reminding us that Christ Himself meets His struggling people right where they are:

> If Jesus is dead today, and rotting in the grave some-where, then these promises aren't worth the paper they're printed on. But, if Jesus is risen from the dead, and if He's alive forevermore the way He says He is, then these promises mean that as a follower of Jesus Christ I can take the word *alone* and permanently remove it from my vocabulary.[4]

Christ actually stands with believers in their pain.[5] He also uses the physical presence of His people to comfort hurting people, as Tom did for us at the hospital. Your compassionate presence can be used by God to help people feel His love.

SUMMARY

I used to work at a homeless shelter in Washington, DC. We had a home for women trying to quit crack cocaine. It is called the Fulton House of Hope. One day I was sitting with the director of the house, Judy Ashburn, when a phone call came in. It was a woman from a wealthy nearby suburb in Virginia. She told Judy that she wanted to send some Christmas gifts to the women at Fulton House. She asked Judy what they might like to receive. "Actually," Judy said, "we can't do that." The woman replied, "What do you mean? Don't they need anything?"

There were, of course, many things the women needed. But Judy didn't want to give the woman an opportunity to make herself feel good by mailing presents over to "those poor crack addicts in the city." Judy understood that the women in her house needed something more than toiletries or clothes. They needed people to encourage them, to pray with them, to be their friends. To be *present*, as Jesus was when He came down from heaven to dwell among us. He didn't do His ministry through the mail. He didn't just send us His blessings and stay safe and warm in His Father's house.

"Here's what you can do," Judy told the woman on the phone. "Why don't you join us for dinner and Bible study on Wednesday night? After you've spent the night getting to know the ladies, then you can give them your gifts."

Real, incarnational ministry requires investment—of your time, your energy, your presence, *yourself*. But without those investments you have not made your love, or God's love, tangible.

QUESTIONS FOR REFLECTION AND DISCUSSION

1. Often we look for the quickest, most efficient way to do things. But taking time to be with someone opens doors for conversation and builds relationship. How could you do more of that?
2. When did someone invest time generously in you? What was the impact?
3. Think about the charities, ministries, or nonprofits you contribute to. How personally engaged are they with the people they serve?

CHAPTER 8

PROACTIVITY

To be a Christian is to move toward need, not comfort.[1]

JOHN PIPER

The LORD said, "I have surely seen the affliction of my people who are in Egypt. . . . I know their sufferings, and I have come down to deliver them."

EXODUS 3:7-8

I find tremendous joy in interviewing new members of our church. They meet with the elders and tell us how they came to faith in Christ. Recently I noticed that many of them became believers after someone pursued them. Only God can convert someone's heart, of course. But I was struck by how many people learn about Christ and trust in Him as a result of the loving, proactive pursuit of other believers.

One woman was invited to church when she was eight years old by a friend on her swim team. A young man who knew nothing about Jesus learned about Him when a guy from a campus ministry kept visiting his dorm room week after week. A woman from El Salvador was invited to church by a neighbor from Finland for five years before the gospel got through to her. But it did get through, because God used the *proactive* love of one of His children.

PROACTIVE, ACCOMMODATING KINDNESS

God does not meet our needs from a distance. Nor does He expect us to reach up to Him. He descended to us, proactively. To be proactive you must study the needs of those you serve and adapt your ministry to their needs. The apologetic of mercy requires us to be accommodating. John Calvin liked to say that God continually accommodates Himself to us. He called the Bible God's "baby talk,"[2] because God speaks to us in ways our finite minds can understand. God knows us and loves us, so He meets us where we are.

I see this proactive kindness in David's treatment of Mephibosheth (see 2 Samuel 9). Mephibosheth was the son of David's best friend, Jonathan, but also the grandson of David's enemy, Saul. David could have seen Mephibosheth as a threat. Another king might have killed everyone associated with King Saul. (We have African refugees in our church who fled for their lives when a new ruler tried to wipe out all supporters of the previous ruler.) David, however, saw an opportunity for God's compassion to be displayed in a public way. "And the king said, 'Is there not still someone of the house of Saul, *that I may show the kindness of God to him?*' Ziba said to the king, 'There is still a son of Jonathan; he is crippled in his feet'" (verse 3, emphasis added).

David showed the "kindness of God" to this disabled man—in both word and deed. In a culture that assumed the disabled must have done something to deserve their affliction, David extended mercy proactively. As a result, Mephibosheth "ate at David's table, like one of the king's sons" (verse 11).

There is a lesson in this for the church. We dare not say to the disabled, "You are welcome to worship with us, if you can walk up the stairs." We must not tell the hard of hearing, "Sit up front so you can hear better." The church is incomplete, handicapped even, if it does not include people with such needs.

If the church is to imitate the Compassionate One, if we are to show the world God's accommodating kindness, we must accommodate ourselves to human need—just as He does. That means building ramps for wheelchairs, providing audio equipment for the hard of hearing, large-print hymnals, elevators, and so on. Many churches resist these investments in their buildings because they are expensive. Well, the blood of Christ was very expensive, but He poured it out willingly because that's what we needed! Christ's body should be inclined to change to meet the needs we encounter, rather than asking the needy to adapt to us.

And if we don't have congregants who are among the underprivileged, perhaps we should do something to invite them in. I remember a deacon meeting at our church when we were studying the priority God puts on ministry to widows, passages such as Acts 6, where the office of deacon was created to care for widows, and James 1:27, "Religion that God our Father accepts as pure and faultless is this: to look after orphans and widows in their distress and to keep oneself from being polluted by the world" (NIV).

God clearly felt that widows were an important demographic for the church to serve. But our church faced a problem with this: We didn't have any widows. We had four hundred people but no widows. In fact, only a handful of our people were over seventy years old. What did we do? We could have said, "Well, if God wants us to serve widows He'll have to send them to us." Instead, we decided to *import widows*. We bought a handicapped-accessible bus, found two facilities across town where five hundred seniors lived, and started bringing folks to church. Today we have a thriving ministry to seniors. Many have become members of the church and found ways to serve others. Our members lead Bible studies at those facilities, and the residents invite nonbelieving friends to worship and special services.

We have learned two lessons from all this: First, ministry is best when it is done within the church community. We bring the residents to church where they became members of our community and engage with the entire body. I believe that the local church is the best place to do word and deed ministry, because it is a family. The second thing we learned is that we had to *move proactively*. Those seniors weren't coming to us. We had to go to them, because that is how God serves us, through *proactive mercy*.

THE MERCIFUL, PROACTIVE PURSUIT OF GOD

You and I do not deserve mercy. As much as we try to live independently of God and anyone else, we are all helpless and undeserving. That's what makes His pursuit of us *merciful* and *proactive.* He does not wait for us to clean up our act or come searching for Him. He comes and finds us right where we are, playing in the mud and pretending He doesn't exist (see Romans 3:10-12).

For this reason, Christians dare not say, "Well, those people in jail deserve to be there, so why should we do ministry there?" I'm ashamed to admit that a former member of my church spent a year in jail before I wrote to him. Sure, he deserves to be in there for what he did. But he doesn't deserve to be forgotten or ignored.

We all deserve condemnation, yet the God of mercy sought us out (see Romans 5:6-8; 1 Peter 3:18). We don't deserve to be invited to His house, yet we have seats at the Father's table where we dine as the King's sons and daughters. Because we are His children, God expects us to seek out others and invite them to the table, as David did for Mephibosheth.

God models this proactive mercy clearly in Scripture. It nearly shouts from passages such as Hosea 2:12-20, which is quoted below. I've inserted five headings in the text to help you see how the merciful and proactive pursuit of God toward undeserving people leads to an exclusive, secure, personal relationship with Him:

1. Human Problem: Sin Made Israel Undeserving

> I will lay waste her vines and her fig trees. . . . I will make
> them a forest, and the beasts of the field shall devour

them. And I will punish her for the feast days of the Baals when she burned offerings to them and adorned herself with her ring and jewelry, and went after her lovers and forgot me, declares the Lord. (verses 12-13)

2. God's Response: Merciful Pursuit

Therefore,[3] behold, I will allure her, and bring her into the wilderness, and speak tenderly to her. And there I will give her her vineyards and make the Valley of Achor a door of hope. And there she shall answer as in the days of her youth, as at the time when she came out of the land of Egypt. (verses 14-15)

3. Result 1: An Exclusive Relationship

And in that day, declares the Lord, you will call me "My Husband," and no longer will you call me "My Baal." For I will remove the names of the Baals from her mouth, and they shall be remembered by name no more. And I will make for them a covenant on that day with the beasts of the field, the birds of the heavens, and the creeping things of the ground. (verses 16-18)

4. Result 2: A Secure Relationship

And I will abolish the bow, the sword, and war from the land, and I will make you lie down in safety. And I will betroth

you to me forever. I will betroth you to me in righteousness
and in justice, in steadfast love and in mercy. I will betroth
you to me in faithfulness. (verses 18-20)

5. Result 3: A Relationship Grounded in Personal Knowledge

And you shall know the LORD. (verse 20)

AGAPE LOVE DRAWS US TOWARD NEED

A homeless woman approached me on the streets of DC one
day. She asked for money but did not look me in the face. She
was looking past me, at the ground. I reached out to shake her
hand. "Hi, I'm Chris. What's your name?" The woman looked
up, startled. She said, "Janet," and burst into tears.

I didn't get an explanation for her tears, but I suspect it was
something like this: After years of being overlooked and unwor-
thy of notice, she had finally been treated like a person. The
simple touch of a hand and exchange of names seemed to break
down walls of emotion in Janet.

Now, I'm not the Good Samaritan. I gave Janet a granola
bar and prayed with her for a few minutes. But even those small
gestures were more than the priest and the Levite did for the
man on the road to Jericho (see Luke 10:25-37). These religious
leaders were supposed to serve God and His people. Yet, when
presented with an opportunity to show God's compassion, they
said they didn't have time. They were too busy being religious to
actually be useful to God. Their positions and desire for personal

safety got in the way of their true callings. I do that too, sometimes, because I'm so self-centered. I need Jesus to make me more like Him, a man with "a mind full of someone else."[4]

That's a great description of Jesus, isn't it? He is the most other-centered person who has ever existed. He is "the founder and perfecter of our faith, who for the joy that was set before him endured the cross" (Hebrews 12:2). What was "the joy" that He yearned for so strongly that He would die to get it? *You!* As He hung on the cross, His mind was filled with thoughts about *you*.

When you get that, when His love has gripped your heart and you recognize you did nothing to deserve it, then God can help you be more like Him. You'll ask Him to help you put the needs of others before your own, to help you move into broken lives and desperate situations, because you know Jesus can do something about it through you. That, says author Art Lindsley, is the essence of *agape* love: "Agape is unmotivated by any moral beauty in the one who is loved, while *eros* (romantic love) and *philia* (friendship) are motivated by beauty or virtue in the loved one. Agape love gives without any desire for something in return."[5]

Agape love draws us toward need, not comfort. It is an alien altruism that testifies to the existence of the One who loves proactively.[6] God calls us to proactive, *agap*e-filled mercy ministry so hurting people will know Him. As we pour our attention and compassion into others, we ask God to open their hearts, to open a channel of compassion that flows from Him, through us.

Consider two of the parables in Luke 15, the lost sheep and the prodigal son. Jesus first described a shepherd who went out to look for one of his sheep, leaving behind the other ninety-nine. Did Jesus say the shepherd went looking for that one sheep because it was the most beautiful of the flock? Because it was his favorite? No. It was the love of the shepherd that prompted him to go searching, not any quality of the sheep.

That's the difference between *eros* and *agape* love. It is *eros* when I love others because they are lovely. It is *agape* when I love them because I am loving. It was *agape* love — other-centered, proactive love — that drove the shepherd out to rescue that sheep. It was *agape* love that drove the Good Shepherd to come down here to rescue you and me.

Jesus also tells the story of the prodigal son in Luke 15. Do you recall what the son did to deserve forgiveness? How he earned the father's acceptance?

He did nothing at all. The young man came home because he was starving and needy, not to restore the relationship with his father. He expected to be treated like a hired hand, not a son. Yes, he did plan to repent, but hunger drove him to repentance. And then, even before he had a chance to *ask* for forgiveness, his father *ran* to him and showered him with kisses of forgiveness. The father ran to him simply because he loved his son.

That's how God loves you. God the Father loves us, not because we deserve it, but because *He is love.* He loves us with proactive *agape* love. "God demonstrates his own love for us in this: While we were still sinners, Christ died for us" (Romans 5:8, NIV).

SUMMARY

Do you remember the band of orphans in *Oliver Twist*? Their poverty drove them into the streets to take what they could get from others. God is calling us to do the opposite. We are orphans whom God has made sons and daughters, paupers whom God has made princes and princesses. Our newfound wealth should drive us into the streets to give what we have to others.

QUESTIONS FOR REFLECTION AND DISCUSSION

1. Why is it important to remember that Jesus saved you by grace, not because you deserved it (see Ephesians 2:1-10)? How should that fact affect your service to others?
2. How could you be more proactive in pointing people to Christ?
3. Does your church congregation reflect the demographics of your community? How might you reach out to those who aren't currently there on Sunday mornings?

CHAPTER 9

YES, YOU

I believe more and more that this is truly the central task of the Christian: to give the Lord the opportunity to exhibit his existence.[1]

FRANCIS SCHAEFFER

Be wise in the way you act toward outsiders; make the most of every opportunity.

COLOSSIANS 4.5, NIV

Jacqueline Liedel was one of the seniors who joined our church after we sent our bus to her building, as I described in the last chapter. Jacqueline is full of energy, spunk, and passion for the Lord. She has some health problems, of course. What eighty-three-year-old doesn't? A month after she had a hip replacement, the changing seasons hit her with a lung infection. I went to see her in the hospital. As we sat and talked, the other patient in the room, a young woman named Rosita, cried out softly every minute or so, in pain.

"It was really irritating the first night," Jacqueline told me.

"But then I got up at three a.m. and spoke to her. I touched her face and prayed for her. Then she quieted down."

One of the nurses had come in while Jacqueline was praying for Rosita. She told Jacqueline, "Maybe that's why you got a lung infection. So you could be in this room, for her." After that, Jacqueline was no longer annoyed by Rosita's nighttime moans and groans. She realized she was there for a purpose.

The day after my visit, Jacqueline called to say her lung infection looked like pneumonia, so they were keeping her for several more days. She had also learned Rosita was supposed to be on another floor. "But they don't have space for her down there," Jacqueline told me. "Where?" I asked. "The end-of-life floor. That's where she's supposed to be. I don't know what to do, Little Brother." That's what Jacqueline calls me. I like it.

I didn't know sickle cell was a fatal disease, that it could take a twenty-four-year-old woman with a six-year-old son. Jacqueline was surprised too. "What do I say to her? I don't know what I'm supposed to do."

I told Jacqueline, "Jesus' body is in heaven now. He is using your hands to love Rosita. So just spend time with her. Tell her about Him, and let Him use you to comfort her."

The next day, I went back to the hospital. Jacqueline held Rosita's hand while I read Psalm 18. We talked about how encouraging it is that our cries for mercy reach God's ears, that God is never too busy to listen and respond to calls for help. We talked about heaven, and Christ, and salvation. And then Rosita smiled as she prayed to receive Christ. It was all God's work. He put Jacqueline in that room and brought me to visit. He worked in the heart of a dying young woman to help her see her sin and need for a Savior. God alone saved her soul. But He let Jacqueline and me be a part of His work.[2]

GOD CAN USE YOU

Jacqueline was nervous about moving into Rosita's life. I'm sure many of you can relate. Perhaps you feel God can't use you in significant ways. Maybe you feel untrained or too ordinary to make a difference in someone's life. If you are God's child, however, you are an instrument He can use for His purposes (see 1 Corinthians 1:26-31).

Do you remember how God used that little slave girl in the household of Naaman the leper (see 2 Kings 5)? Most people think children have little power or influence. But God did powerful things through that seemingly unimportant girl. Notice the clear contrast between the "great man" and this "little girl":

> Naaman, commander of the army of the king of Syria, was *a great man* with his master and in high favor, because by him the LORD had given victory to Syria. He was a mighty man of valor, but he was a leper. Now the Syrians on one of their raids had carried off *a little girl* from the land of Israel, and she worked in the service of Naaman's wife. She said to her mistress, "Would that my lord were with the prophet who is in Samaria! He would cure him of his leprosy." (verses 1-3, emphasis added)

Naaman was powerful and rich. The girl was powerless and penniless. He was a general with great freedom. She was a slave with no freedom. The girl had little of her own to offer Naaman. Yet, she had faith when much of Israel had abandoned the worship of *Yahweh* and chased after foreign gods. She knew about the prophet Elisha and confidently told her mistress he could heal Naaman. At a time when Israel had failed to be "a light for the nations" (Isaiah 49:6), this young girl became a light of hope in Damascus. It wasn't her light. She simply reflected the light of God's truth in a dark place so that Naaman could see.

Are you outnumbered by nonbelievers in your neighborhood, school, family, or workplace? Remember that as a member of God's household, you are His instrument. You are not alone. Wherever you are now, know that you don't have to be a big shot or have all the answers to the problems of those around you. That Israelite girl did not know how to cure leprosy, but she knew where to point Naaman. As God's child, she was tapped into the Source of all healing and hope, and that made her useful to God right where she was. How about you?

OPEN YOUR EYES AND YOUR HEART

God is calling some of His children to move overseas to bring healing and hope to the slums and dark places of the world. Many of us, however, are called to remain right where we are.

Perhaps you are living in a nice community in the suburbs. It's not wrong to live there. But it *is* wrong to let your comfortable life insulate you from the needs of people around you.[3]

YES, YOU   111

Next Saturday before you take your children to soccer practice or the playground, why not ask God how He could use you there?

Maybe you are a student or work in an office somewhere. What if you prayed for the people you see every week and asked the Lord to open doors into their lives? I guarantee some of them are struggling with something right now. You carry the light of the world with you (see Matthew 5:14-16)! Don't smother it, because there are needy people everywhere, even if they don't appear to have needs.

Today, Christianity is growing dramatically among the world's poorest people. They know their need. The wealthy, on the other hand, often fail to see how Jesus is relevant to their lives. That's the point Jesus makes in Mark 10:25: "It is easier for a camel to go through the eye of a needle than for a rich person to enter the kingdom of God." Did Jesus mean that the door of heaven is closed to the rich? Of course not. The rich are just better cushioned from reality; they don't know how needy they truly are. Do you know anyone like that?

In His mercy, God sometimes creates a vacuum of need in otherwise comfortable lives. In that vacuum, many become desperate enough to shed their pride and seek a Savior. That's what happened to Naaman, who was cushioned from the reality of the world and the sin in his heart. But when that proud, successful man ran out of options, his hopelessness drove him into the arms of God.

I think the materially comfortable—the Naamans of today—could actually be another unreached people group, right under our noses. They drive expensive cars, wear nice clothes, and appear to be happy. But many are miserable. Driving home in a BMW or Suburban doesn't make it easier to face a crumbling marriage. Living in a big house doesn't help your teenager get off drugs. A large bank account is little comfort when Alzheimer's slowly steals your spouse from you.[4]

Material comfort and earthly success can be like Bubble Wrap, protecting people from the hard reality of their situation: "For you say, I am rich, I have prospered, and I need nothing, not realizing that you are wretched, pitiable, poor, blind, and naked" (Revelation 3:17). To remove the obstacles of wealth and prosperity, God sometimes allows problems to creep into the lives of comfortable people. Those problems make them hungry for help and for answers. So open your eyes and your heart, and let God use you to serve those hungry souls the Bread of Life.

IT'S OKAY TO FEEL HELPLESS

Maybe you are still unconvinced that you, right where you are today, can be used by God to reveal His mercy and truth. If so, let me show you something else: the way Jesus trained His unqualified disciples to do ministry. The miracle of the feeding of the five thousand appears in all four gospels, so you have probably heard the story. But did you notice that Jesus gave the disciples an impossible command and then showed them how to obey it?

Before we look at that command, let me remind you of the clear connection that Jesus made between spiritual and material needs. This is a word and deed event. In Mark's account we learn that Jesus had compassion on the crowd, not because they forgot their lunch, but "because they were like sheep without a shepherd. And he began to teach them many things" (6:34).

It was their need for a shepherd, *for Him*, that aroused His compassion. The miracle was a teaching tool for both the crowd and the disciples. Jesus taught the crowd that He was a shepherd worth following, because He could meet their needs. Not merely the needs of their bellies, but of their souls. By feeding so many with so little, Jesus revealed Himself as the same God who fed His people in the wilderness years before[5] and was now with them once again.

But He wouldn't be with them for long. Jesus knew He would soon leave His ministry in the hands of eleven men who didn't seem to have it all together. He had to teach the disciples how to minister to the needy and the lost. They had to know how to feed His sheep in the coming days, when He wouldn't be with them physically.

The first thing they had to know was that they couldn't do it alone. When Jesus told the apostles, "You give them something to eat" (Mark 6:37), He knew it was impossible for them to do it. Jesus wanted the disciples to feel the helplessness of staring thousands of hungry people in the face and not having enough food to feed them. Don't we feel the same sense of helplessness as we look at the overwhelming needs of the world today?

Here's my point: Feelings of helplessness should not be obstacles to ministry, but reasons to cling to Christ. Just as need drives unbelievers like Naaman into the arms of God, our helplessness keeps us coming back to Him as we do His ministry:

> It is a good thing for us to know how very poor we are, and how far from being able to meet the wants of the people around us. It is for our good to be made to confess this in so many words to our Lord. Truly, he who writes this comment has often felt as if he had neither loaf nor fish, and yet for some forty years and more he has been a full-handed waiter at the King's great banquets.[6]

Jesus' next lesson was to deploy the disciples as waiters to distribute the food. He didn't lay out a buffet for the people. He could have simply snapped His fingers, made a huge table, and asked everyone to file through. Instead, He offered thanks to His Father and gave the bread and fish "to the disciples to set before the people" (Mark 6:41).

It's fascinating to me that Jesus did not explain things to the disciples first. He could have said, "All right, look. I know there's only a little bread and fish. But as you hand it out, I'm going to make it regenerate. There'll be plenty, so don't worry." Why didn't He explain the plan?

I think Jesus wanted the disciples to trust and rely on Him to do the impossible (which is just what you need to do when you move into the lives of hurting people around you). As the disciples walked around like waiters, trusting Jesus that somehow there would be food enough for all, they experienced the miracle firsthand. They saw the bread multiply in their hands, they saw the empty bellies fill up, and their faith in Jesus grew. They learned they could do impossible things when Jesus was with them.

When the disciples had counted to seven (five loaves of bread plus two fish), they felt helpless. They knew they could never feed the crowd with those seven items. But Jesus was teaching *kingdom of God algebra* to His disciples. In the regular world, $5 + 2 = 7$. But in the kingdom, where x equals Christ, $5 + 2 + x = 5,000$. Through this miracle, the disciples learned to count to eight: five loaves of bread plus two fish *plus Jesus*.

If you are trying to do something that seems impossible and you feel frustrated or hopeless, perhaps you are relying on yourself and earthly resources. Learn to count to eight. Take whatever resources you have, then ask Jesus to use them however He wants. If He has called you to do something difficult, you can be sure He will provide all that you need to do it.

SUMMARY

Are you available to be used by Jesus? Maybe you are afraid of what you might lose—friendship, time, security, the respect of others. Yet, there are people around you right now with wounds and hurts God can address through you. Some are lost souls whom God can save when they hear the gospel.

Some people, like Naaman, are good at hiding their needs behind nice clothes and comfortable lives. Pay attention at school, at work, at the pool, and in the neighborhood. You could be a messenger to hurting people there. Get close enough to folks to find out where they hurt, and be their friend. Tell them about the only Source of real healing for bodies and souls.

No one is too far outside God's household to be invited inside. And all His children are equipped to make that invitation. As you step out to do ministry, you will sometimes feel as bewildered as the disciples handing out bread. You will also learn how draining it is to serve others. That's what the next chapter is about—how to stay tapped into the Vine for nourishment and encouragement so you can bear His fruit without burning out.

QUESTIONS FOR REFLECTION OR DISCUSSION

1. Why do wounds cause people to isolate themselves from other people and God?

2. Do you know wealthy, successful, comfortable people who do not know Jesus? They may be good at hiding their needs, but they have them. What if you or your church started a ministry for people struggling to care for their elderly parents? Or a substance-abuse program? A divorce support group?

3. If you are unsure how to show someone Christ's love, here are three practical ideas. Have you found others?
   • *Listen.* Be a compassionate audience who does not judge or try to fix other people. You have no idea how many people long for a kind person who will just listen to them share and cry.

- *Pray for God's comfort.* Ask the Holy Spirit to use His power and your presence to grant comfort and peace to your friend's heart.
- *Do kind deeds and don't take the credit.* Even the most cynical person is touched by kind deeds. Use those deeds as a way to tell about God's kindness to you in Christ.

CHAPTER 10

ABIDING

I am the vine; you are the branches. Whoever abides in me and I in him, he it is that bears much fruit, for apart from me you can do nothing.

JOHN 15:5

My God will supply every need of yours according to his riches in glory in Christ Jesus.

PHILIPPIANS 4:19

Until 2008, my wife and I were quite comfortable. We had a good marriage, healthy children, and a nice home. We were both heavily invested in ministry at our church. Then the Lord used stage 3 breast cancer, multiple surgeries, chemotherapy, and radiation to shake things up. It was a long, hard year. In 2010, Sara had a local recurrence. In the spring of 2013 we learned the cancer had moved to her brain. She will be on chemotherapy for the rest of her life.

Why do I tell you this? Because you must never forget that you need God as much as anyone else. Through Sara's cancer, God has taught both of us how necessary it is to abide in Him daily. Not only for our sake, so we don't burn out, but also so our ministry to others is authentic and points people to Christ.

God has used Sara in some powerful ways since cancer entered her story. Not long ago, a woman in our church was diagnosed with cancer. I met with her and her husband and we prayed, because that's what pastors should do. But Sara did something I could never do.

Sara found out when Trina's first chemo appointment was. Then Sara scheduled her own weekly chemo to happen on the same day, in the same room. Sara got there early. She brought flowers to brighten the room and taped Scripture verses on the walls. She brought ginger ale for nausea and Jolly Rancher candies for dry mouth. Then, she and Trina sat next to one another, two IV bags hanging between them, talking as they received chemo together.

YOU HAVE TO BE FED TO FEED OTHERS

God has done other great things through Sara. She started a cancer support group at our church and is sought out by people with other medical crises. But God can do these things *through* Sara only because of the things He is doing *in* Sara.

People often tell her, "Oh what great faith you have! You are so strong!" She replies, "It's God who is great. Not me, not my faith. Where else can I go? I have no other options. I *have* to run to Him!"[1]

Sara was scared, not strong. The essence of faith is not

inner strength; it is the recognition that we are weak and cling to a strong God (see 2 Corinthians 4:7; 11:24–12:10). Cancer made Sara aware of her true weakness. Humbled and fearful, she ran to the Lord because no one else could help. The strength and encouragement she shares with others is not her own, but is the overflow of what she receives from the "Father of mercies and God of all comfort" (1:3).

Sara is a credible guide to people who suffer because, as she says, "No one likes to be led through a desert by someone who hasn't been through one." Don't get me wrong. I am not saying you can't minister to cancer patients unless you've had cancer. What I am saying is that you are a more credible guide if you have faced your own challenges and learned to abide in Christ during them.

When I was a lieutenant in the army, we had a rule, "Leaders eat last." It is a good rule, because it ensures the troops get what they need first. Plus, seeing their sergeants and officers standing at the back of the line at every meal reminds soldiers that their leaders care about their well-being. In ministry, however, the opposite is true: *Leaders must eat first.* If we are going to have anything to give, if we are going to do ministry in God's name and power rather than our own, we have to acknowledge our own hunger and need.[2] We must be fed from above before we can feed others.[3]

Ministry is draining and difficult. To be sustained in it, and to do it for the right reasons, we must be tapped into the Source of mercy ourselves. Otherwise we do ministry with earthly strength, for earthly motives, with only earthly results.

DON'T WASTE YOUR THIRST

During his battle with prostate cancer, John Piper wrote a little book with a huge message. *Don't Waste Your Cancer*[4] is not only for people with cancer. It is for anyone who struggles. Piper shares how God uses trials and trauma to teach us to abide in Him.

"You will waste your cancer if you think that 'beating' cancer means staying alive—rather than cherishing Christ."[5] Read that again. Do you see what Piper is saying? If we put our hope merely in surviving the cancer, or in getting that job, or in passing that exam, we are missing something precious. Piper is saying that growth in the love and knowledge of Christ *is the purpose* of a trial (see Philippians 1:21).

When we feel drained and burdened, God wants us to cast our cares and burdens on Him. If we miss this opportunity to grow in our dependency on Him, we waste an opportunity for growth—even if we *are* physically healed, or get the job, or pass the exam. God intends to root us more deeply in Christ, so we will be more firmly planted for future storms. He also wants to make us more useful instruments for His glory.

This is a critical lesson for anyone involved in ministry. If we only help people find solutions to problems, then we aren't really doing *ministry* at all. God allows challenge and hardship in our lives for a reason: to make us run to Christ (see Philippians 3:8; 2 Corinthians 1:9). How does that happen? By looking to Christ and learning from Him, instead of looking elsewhere for help.

Another gem from Piper: "We waste our cancer if we spend too much time reading about cancer and not enough time reading about God."[6] When you face a serious illness you will be tempted to spend hours on medical websites rather than meditating on God's Word. If your struggle is financial, then financial magazines and spreadsheets beckon with promises to help. And they might help—with your financial problem. What about your anxiety? If problems don't drive you to God's Word, you fail to learn what God says about resting in Him.

God leads His people into deserts because He loves us. Sometimes that desert is the emptiness we feel as we pour ourselves out in service to others. Sometimes it is our own hardship. In either case, God wants us to learn to bring our thirsty souls to His Word and drink it in deeply (see Deuteronomy 8:3).

THE WORD OF GOD IS LIVING WATER

Psalm 1 gives us a description of how we can survive and thrive during periods of spiritual drought:

> Blessed is the one
>   who does not walk in step with the wicked
> or stand in the way that sinners take
>   or sit in the company of mockers,
> but whose delight is in the law of the LORD,
>   and who meditates on his law day and night.
> That person is like a tree planted by streams of water,
>   which yields its fruit in season
> and whose leaf does not wither—
>   whatever they do prospers.

Not so the wicked!
    They are like chaff
    that the wind blows away.
Therefore the wicked will not stand in the judgment,
    nor sinners in the assembly of the righteous.
For the LORD watches over the way of the righteous,
    but the way of the wicked leads to destruction. (NIV)

Like John 15, this psalm describes what it looks like to abide in Christ. I think Jesus must have had Psalm 1 in mind when He said,

I am the vine; you are the branches. Whoever abides in me and I in him, he it is that bears much fruit, for apart from me you can do nothing. If anyone does not abide in me he is thrown away like a branch and withers; and the branches are gathered, thrown into the fire, and burned. (John 15:5-6)

The psalmist and Jesus describe two types of people, those who abide in the Lord and bear fruit, and those who dry up because they reject fellowship with the Lord. He is the Source of power, of energy, of nutrients. We are branches that receive these things, and our ministry only bears fruit when we abide in Him. Fruit does not depend on our performance, obedience, or cleverness. Fruit comes from *connection* to Christ. The person in Psalm 1 is blessed because he sinks his roots into the Word of God, all the time.

I know it is hard to make time for daily Bible study. Other things often seem more urgent. But think of this: The Creator of the universe actually wrote this *to you* for a purpose: to sanctify you and cleanse you and nourish you. The Word of God is living water (see Ephesians 5:26).

Consider the importance of water to life. People can live for many days without food, but after seventy-two hours without water, they die. In the Old Testament rain is frequently called a blessing from God. Without rain, your crops do not grow; you can't feed your family or barter for things. Rain and water were life to the people of Israel.

Psalm 1:3 says the blessed person is "planted" by streams of water. To the Israelites, who depended upon rain for their survival in a dry land, these words about being planted by — actually living right next to — "streams of water" must have sounded like a description of paradise! And they are:

> The river of the water of life, bright as crystal, flowing from the throne of God and of the Lamb through the middle of the street of the city; also, on either side of the river, the tree of life with its twelve kinds of fruit, yielding its fruit each month. The leaves of the tree were for the healing of the nations. (Revelation 22:1-2)

The water of life feeds the tree of life that bears leaves of healing and abundant fruit, fruit that ripens not once a year but every month! That's the power of the water flowing from the throne of God and of the Lamb. This is the same living water

Jesus told the Samaritan woman about in John 4. It is the source of life itself.

LIVING WATER FOR A DYING WORLD

Ezekiel had a vision about this living water flowing in a river from the throne of God. It is called living water because it brings life: "Swarms of living creatures will live wherever the river flows. There will be large numbers of fish, because this water flows there and *makes the salt water fresh*; so where the river flows everything will live" (Ezekiel 47:9, NIV, emphasis added).

The Lamb of God is the Source of life. Jesus offers living water that can turn salty water into fresh water—ashes into beauty, mourning into joy, and despair into praise (see Isaiah 61:3). Everyone who knows Christ is a tree planted by that river and a branch on His vine. However, we can be one of God's trees or branches and not experience much fruit. The pain and misery of this world constantly war against our ability to rest in our salvation, to believe in the coming world where Christ will right all wrongs.

How do we experience a fruitful life in a painful world like this? How do we encourage the downtrodden? I'm not speaking at this point about salvation, about choosing the path of the righteous, as in Psalm 1. If you are in Christ, you possess His righteousness and are firmly planted by that stream forever and ever. Yet, you can dwell in God's garden and not bear much fruit. Look again at what Jesus said about the source of fruit: "I am the vine; you are the branches. *Whoever abides* in me and

I in him, *he it is* that bears much fruit, for apart from me you can do nothing" (John 15:5, emphasis added).

Jesus wants us to bear fruit in abundance, even in times of struggle and hardship. That can happen if we find our rest and nourishment in Him at all times. When we learn this lesson for ourselves, we have more to offer the suffering people we serve.

COME TO THE WATERS

Not long ago, we had a very dry year in Virginia. We lost some azaleas in our backyard because we didn't water them, and they dried up and died. We also had a more serious problem. Our big trees were so thirsty during the drought that they sucked the soil dry around our house, causing our home's foundation to fall a couple of inches. This opened up cracks in our drywall and made our doors stick. An engineer explained how a tree can send roots far and wide to find more water. Thirst is a powerful force.

I was very thirsty back in 2008 as we dealt with Sara's cancer treatment. I had not learned the lessons that I've been sharing throughout this chapter. I thought that year was a *physical* challenge. I just had to do more household chores and keep life in order so Sara could get naps and go to numerous medical appointments. Then there were the everyday challenges of working at the church while raising three young children in a house that always needs something repaired or replaced. I thought I could manage on my own if I just tried hard enough.

I didn't realize I was being so independent until I began to feel the strain. I felt tightness in my chest and a queasy pain in my stomach that Rolaids couldn't take away. A general feeling of anxiety and stress plagued me every day, but I just kept plugging away. I was in self-reliant survival mode, completely missing the lesson God wanted to teach me that year. To find relief I worked harder to clear items off my to-do list. I hoped that getting more things done would bring me rest, that if I could just accomplish a little more one week, the next week would be easier.

I walked around most of the time on the edge of overwhelming panic, but still tried harder to cope in my own strength. I had strayed from the stream of living water and therefore felt dry and fruitless. I wasn't drinking from the stream like the person in Psalm 1. My roots were not in the right soil.

Finally, one Sunday in August, I went to worship at another church, where I had no duties to distract me. I heard the answer for my thirsty soul when the worship leader opened with Isaiah 55:

> Come, all you who are thirsty,
>   come to the waters;
> and you who have no money,
>   come, buy and eat!
> Come, buy wine and milk
>   without money and without cost.
> Why spend money on what is not bread,
>   and your labor on what does not satisfy?
> Listen, listen to me, and eat what is good,
>   and you will delight in the richest of fare.

Give ear and come to me;
> listen, that you may live. (Isaiah 55:1-3, NIV)

Oh, how my soul opened up when I heard those words! I had no idea how thirsty I was, how much I needed Jesus. The effort of caring for Sara had sucked the moisture out of the soil around my soul. I had been so thirsty, yet my own efforts to survive away from the stream had only increased my thirst. Finally, God's Word revealed how thirsty and hungry I was, and that only Jesus could feed me.

The Lord's Supper was served later in that service. Clutching my bread and cup of wine, I sat for a long time, treasuring that intimate moment. Empty and deeply aware of my need, I knew that Jesus was there with me. He came to pour Himself into me, to fill up my dry and empty places.

Jesus fed my soul that day, and it was indeed good. The knot in my stomach, that painful, anxious feeling in my chest—they just melted away. In the following weeks I found I was still able to rest in Him. I started my days in prayer and the Word instead of reviewing my to-do list. As a result I bore more of His fruit in the way I lived. I became more patient and kind. I smiled more, and when people commented on that, I gave credit to God. Because it was Christ I had been thirsty for all along.

SUMMARY

Contrast two hypothetical "servants" who volunteer at a soup kitchen. Bill looks ordinary on the outside, well-dressed but nondescript. On the inside, his heart shows the scars of his sin and the stitches of grace. God has shown Bill the emptiness in his soul and filled him with redeeming love. The joy of his salvation makes him eager to serve others, just as God served him. When Bill sits and eats with the homeless men at the soup kitchen, they relate to one another as broken men who need the same Carpenter.

Ted is also well-dressed and unremarkable in appearance. He comes to the same soup kitchen once a year at Thanksgiving. Ted helps in the kitchen for a few hours, nods at Bill, and then climbs back in his warm car feeling good about himself. Is there any hint of mutual suffering in Ted's service? Will his annual visit cause others to ask, "What is the reason for your love and hope?"

People are drawn to people like Bill, and Jesus, because they are *real*. Jesus lived a real life that contained hunger and sadness and suffering. People around us who suffer are going to respond to our ministry if we are real and speak about our own neediness. Paul understood that: "Not that we are sufficient in ourselves to claim anything as coming from us, but our sufficiency is from God" (2 Corinthians 3:5). To be certain we don't become a surrogate savior, we must "lead with a limp,"[7] saying to people, "Come with me to the cross, where we will *both* find healing." Humble, sacrificial service by the body will teach the world about a Savior who suffered and saves.

QUESTIONS FOR REFLECTION OR DISCUSSION

1. Prayerfully examine your heart. Where do you seek rest, hope, and encouragement?

2. Can you name a time when you relied on your own strength to do something? How about a time you were forced to rely on God instead? What did you learn from each?

3. When you are tired or frustrated, where do you run? When you are discouraged, what do you do?

4. Is it hard for you to remain planted in God's truth? Where else do you sink your roots?

5. How does your own spiritual health affect the fruitfulness of your ministry and relationships?

CONCLUSION

*Mercy and truth are met together; righteousness and peace
have kissed each other. Truth shall spring out of the earth; and
righteousness shall look down from heaven.*

PSALM 85:10-11, KJV

*Truly, I say to you, in the new world, when the Son of Man will
sit on his glorious throne . . . everyone who has left houses or
brothers or sisters or father or mother or children or lands, for
my name's sake, will receive a hundredfold and will inherit
eternal life.*

MATTHEW 19.20-29

Merciful apologists use both word and deed to help people
know God. We employ each as Jesus did, according to the need
at hand. Jesus never said to His disciples, "Today is a word
ministry day. Let's just do evangelism." He didn't compartmen-
talize His ministry like that and ignore the material needs of
people He encountered on "evangelism days."

We do ministry for the same reason Jesus did—to reveal

who He is so people can enter into a relationship with Him. Only He can save souls. Our duty is to proclaim the gospel clearly and to do good works that will "adorn the doctrine of God" (Titus 2:10).

Jesus was always aware of the spiritual and material needs of the people He encountered. So He employed both word and deed ministry as appropriate, knowing which would be best at the time for that person. Jesus was always focused on people, not ministry techniques.

Today as you employ the apologetic of mercy, the thing that will hold word and deed together is *you*. The relationship you have with people creates the context in which ministry can happen. We don't preach the Word of God at people and remain distant from them. We talk about the Word naturally while traveling or eating or comforting the bereaved—just as Jesus did.

The key thing is to *be with people*. When you are with them, when you have a desire to know them and love them, you can employ words and deeds as needed, when needed.[1]

When we move proactively into the lives of hurting people, bringing with us both earthly and heavenly bread, we address doubts as they arise. That's what apologetics is, after all. It is a response to doubt. Suffering causes everyone to doubt, so you should anticipate it and give God's answer. "Before they call I will answer; while they are yet speaking I will hear" (Isaiah 65:24).

God can use our merciful deeds and words of hope to respond to the suffering and doubt of bodies and souls. But we must act—this book is not theoretical! The body of Christ must move confidently into the lives of doubting people who dwell in painful places, knowing we do not go alone.

NOT OPTIONAL

But we must *go* and *act*. Yes, there is an urgent need for sinners to hear the gospel preached. If, however, we neglect Scripture's clear call to serve suffering people, we face the indignant anger of God. Think, for example, of Sodom. What was the sin of the city of Sodom? What leaps immediately to mind? God might have had something different in mind than you do: "Now this was the sin of your sister Sodom: She and her daughters were arrogant, overfed and unconcerned; they did not help the poor and needy. They were haughty and did detestable things before me. Therefore I did away with them" (Ezekiel 16:49-50, NIV).

"Arrogant, overfed and unconcerned; they did not help the poor and needy." I'm afraid many churches fit this description today. How many Christians wall themselves in from the world to keep themselves safe? If we hide behind walls, won't that also keep the world "safe" from us?

What is the meaning behind Jesus' words in Matthew 16:18: "And I tell you, you are Peter, and on this rock I will build my church, and the gates of hell shall not prevail against it"? Many interpret that last phrase to mean that the church must build strong walls to resist the Enemy, to protect ourselves from the Devil. But is that what a plain reading of the text tells us? Is Jesus saying we have to defend ourselves? I don't think so.

Consider the blessing spoken over Rebekah before she went to marry Isaac: "And they blessed Rebekah and said to her, 'Our sister, may you increase to thousands upon thousands; *may your offspring possess the cities* of their enemies'" (Genesis 24:60, NIV, emphasis added). We, the church, are Rebekah's offspring.[2] Jesus wasn't telling Peter that the church would be a fortress Christians could use to seclude themselves from the world. Instead He was saying that the world and Satan *will not be safe from us.* The church is called to storm the gates of Satan! Christ leads us out into a dark world on a rescue mission to redeem those held in captivity, feed those who hunger, and comfort those who mourn.

TOGETHER, WORD AND DEED REVEAL THE KINGDOM

This is not the way life should be. And this is not the way life will be. We look forward to the restored creation, "a new heaven and a new earth, where righteousness dwells" (2 Peter 3:13, NIV), where God "will wipe every tear from their eyes. There will be no more death or mourning or crying or pain, for the old order of things has passed away" (Revelation 21:4, NIV).

That world is not here yet, so deeds of mercy and words of compassion are like a stargate. For those who haven't seen the *Stargate* movies and TV shows, a stargate allows people to travel to other places and times. Mercy ministry can do something similar, giving people a foretaste of the real, restored world where we will suffer no more.

Jesus preached good news about the kingdom of God[3] and revealed that kingdom to sick and suffering people when He healed them. He applied the laws of God's kingdom to their bodies. We do the same when we provide homes for orphans, food for the hungry, and freedom for the oppressed. This world of pain and death will pass away. For now, we dwell in the time between the Garden and the City, as sojourners traveling through a fallen, broken world. Our deeds of mercy and words of hope open a stargate to help hurting people see creation redeemed and restored:

> When Jesus expels demons and heals the sick, he is driving out of creation the powers of destruction, and is healing and restoring created beings who are hurt and sick. The lordship of God, to which the healings witness, restores sick creation to health. Jesus' healings are not supernatural miracles in a natural world. They are the only truly "natural" things in a world that is unnatural, demonized, and wounded.[4]

The life, death, and resurrection of Jesus kicked off God's global renovation project. We don't experience it all now, and our efforts do not accelerate its completion. For now, we get glimpses, foretastes, of the City to come. When Jesus read from Isaiah 61 in His hometown synagogue, He declared that Isaiah's prophecy of restored creation was being fulfilled. Christ had come in order to:

> Provide for those who grieve in Zion — to bestow on them a crown of beauty instead of ashes, the oil of joy instead of mourning, and a garment of praise instead of a spirit of despair. They will be called oaks of righteousness, a planting of the LORD for the display of his splendor. They will

rebuild the ancient ruins and restore the places long
devastated; they will renew the ruined cities that have
been devastated for generations. (verses 3-4, NIV)

Who will rebuild the ancient ruins and restore the places long devastated? God will, but He uses you and me as His instruments. Jesus said, "As the Father has sent me, even so I am sending you" (John 20:21). Christ continues His ministry through us, His body. We "display His splendor" when we do His work and give Him the glory for it. Those we serve get a foretaste of the heavenly city when devastated areas of their lives are restored and we tell them how to become citizens of that city, in Christ.

His kingdom is real but not fully present, which is why we still experience pain and hardship. Yet, the works of mercy we do are evidence that Jesus is at work, making all things new:

Jesus' miracles were signs of the kingdom, pledges of the
time of the restoration of all things. Our deeds of mercy in
Christ's name do not have the authenticating power of his
miracles, but they do point in hope to the consummation
triumph of God's saving mercy. Our deeds of mercy have a
double implication: they point forward to the promise of
the new heavens and earth; they also show the beginning
of the fulfillment of the promise in the pouring out of the
love of Christ through the Spirit.[5]

You and I get to pour out the love of Christ to the world! How awesome is that? Our deeds of mercy will demonstrate His love and compassion. Our words of truth will declare the gospel and the need for everyone to repent and trust in Christ.

As you get out there and apply what you have learned in this book, would you please share with me your experiences? Visit www.tangibletheology.com/stories and post a comment. You will also find resources, encouragement, and updates from fellow believers who are making the love of God tangible in the world today.

QUESTIONS FOR REFLECTION OR DISCUSSION

1. Read Isaiah 19:22. How does God use suffering? For what purpose?
2. According to Mark 6:34, what was the reason Jesus had compassion on the five thousand people He fed? What are the motivations for compassion today?
3. In your experience, at your church or in organizations you are familiar with, do God's people do a good job of addressing needs in a holistic way?
4. What could be changed to make your ministry more comprehensive, so it addresses head, heart, and body?
5. What will you do differently after finishing this book? Write down three specific things you will do.

RESOURCES

Many of the tools, lectures, and resources we use at Alexandria Presbyterian Church may be found at www.alexandriapres .org/mercy.

My blog provides practical suggestions, examples of tangible ministry, and a list of resources I am always adding to: www .tangibletheology.com.

One of the most helpful resources Sara and I have found is the music of Indelible Grace (www.igracemusic.com). Why is music a resource? Because the lyrics of these old hymns, set to beautiful new music, nourish the soul and comfort the heart. When ministry gets tough and the weight of pain threatens to crush us, Sara and I are led to God's comfort through the music of Indelible Grace.

APOLOGETICS AND EVANGELISM

Boa, Kenneth D. and Robert M. Bowman Jr. *Faith Has Its Reasons: Integrative Approaches to Defending the Christian Faith.* Downers Grove, IL: InterVarsity, 2001.

Conn, Harvie M. *Evangelism: Doing Justice and Preaching Grace*. Phillipsburg, PA: Presbyterian & Reformed, 1992.

Cowan, Stephen B. *Five Views on Apologetics*. Grand Rapids, MI: Zondervan, 2000.

Follis, Bryan. *Truth with Love: The Apologetics of Francis Schaeffer*. Wheaton, IL: Crossway, 2006.

Frame, John. *Apologetics to the Glory of God*. Phillipsburg, PA: Presbyterian & Reformed, 1994.

Lindsley, Art. *Love, the Ultimate Apologetic: The Heart of Christian Witness*. Downers Grove, IL: InterVarsity, 2008.

Miller, Paul. *Love Walked Among Us: Learning to Love Like Jesus*. Colorado Springs, CO: NavPress, 2001.

Schaeffer, Francis A. *The God Who Is There*. Downers Grove, IL: InterVarsity, 1968.

WORD AND DEED MINISTRY

Atkinson, Donald and Charles Roesel. *Meeting Needs, Sharing Christ*. Nashville: LifeWay, 1995.

Bakke, Ray. *A Theology As Big As the City*. Downers Grove, IL: InterVarsity, 1997.

Conn, Harvie M. *Evangelism: Doing Justice and Preaching Grace*. Phillipsburg, PA: Presbyterian & Reformed, 1992.

Conn, Harvie M. and Manuel Ortiz. *Urban Ministry: The Kingdom, the City and the People of God*. Downers Grove, IL: InterVarsity, 2001.

Corbett, Steve and Brian Fikkert. *When Helping Hurts: How to Alleviate Poverty Without Hurting the Poor . . . and Yourself*. Chicago: Moody, 2009.

Keller, Timothy. *Ministries of Mercy: The Call of the Jericho Road.* Phillipsburg, PA: Presbyterian & Reformed, 1997.

Lupton, Robert. *Compassion, Justice and the Christian Life.* Ventura, CA: Regal, 2007.

Olasky, Marvin. *The Tragedy of American Compassion.* Washington, DC: Regnery Publishing, 1992.

Olson, Jeannine. *Calvin and Social Welfare.* Cranbury, NJ: Associated University Presses, 1989.

Ortiz, Manuel and Susan Baker, eds. *The Urban Face of Mission.* Phillipsburg, PA: Presbyterian & Reformed, 2002.

Perkins, John. *Beyond Charity.* Grand Rapids, MI: Baker, 2001.

Perkins, John, ed. *Restoring At-Risk Communities.* Grand Rapids, MI: Baker, 1996.

Sherman, Amy. *Restorers of Hope: Reaching the Poor in Your Community with Church-Based Ministries That Work.* Eugene, OR: Wipf & Stock Publishers, 2004.

Sider, Ron. *Good News and Good Works.* Grand Rapids, MI: Baker, 2004.

Strauch, Alexander. *The New Testament Deacon: The Church's Minister of Mercy.* Colorado Springs, CO: Lewis & Roth Publishers, 1992. (Study guide also available.)

ON SUFFERING

Bonhoeffer, Dietrich. *Letters and Papers from Prison.* New York: Touchstone, 1997.

Bonhoeffer, Dietrich. *Psalms: The Prayer Book of the Bible.* Minneapolis: Augsburg Fortress, 1970.

Guthrie, Nancy, ed. *Be Still, My Soul: Embracing God's Purpose and Provision in Suffering.* Wheaton, IL: Crossway, 2010.

Guthrie, Nancy. *Hearing Jesus Speak into Your Sorrow.* Carol Stream, IL: Tyndale, 2009.

Guthrie, Nancy. *The One Year Book of Hope.* Carol Stream, IL: Tyndale, 2005.

Hallesby, Ole. *Prayer.* Minneapolis: Augsburg Fortress, 1994.

Tiegreen, Chris. *Why a Suffering World Makes Sense.* Grand Rapids, MI: Baker, 2006.

Yancey, Philip. *What Good Is God? In Search of a Faith That Matters.* New York: FaithWords, 2010.

Yancey, Philip. *Where Is God When It Hurts?* Grand Rapids, MI: Zondervan, 1990.

SLAVERY AND HUMAN TRAFFICKING

Batstone, David. *Not for Sale: The Return of the Global Slave Trade—and How We Can Fight It.* New York: HarperOne, 2007.

Haugen, Gary. *Good News about Injustice, Updated 10th Anniversary Edition: A Witness of Courage in a Hurting World.* Downers Grove, IL: InterVarsity, 2009.

Haugen, Gary and Greg Hunter. *Terrify No More: Young Girls Held Captive and the Daring Undercover Operation to Win Their Freedom.* Nashville: W Publishing Group, 2005.

Skinner, E. Benjamin. *A Crime So Monstrous: Face-to-Face with Modern-Day Slavery.* New York: Free Press, 2009.

ORGANIZATIONS AND ONLINE RESOURCES

The Chalmers Center for Economic Development provides research, training, and practical resources: www.chalmers.org.

The Christian Community Development Association exists to inspire, train, and connect Christians who seek to bear witness to the kingdom of God by reclaiming and restoring under-resourced communities: www.ccda.org.

The Christian Reformed Church of Canada offers many mercy ministry resources: www.diaconalministries.com.

The Presbyterian Church in America is actively engaged in disaster response, mercy ministry, and church planting in needy communities: www.pcamna.org.

Youth With A Mission has helpful information, resources, and ministry opportunities on their mercy ministry site: www.ywam-mercy.org.

NOTES

Foreword

1. Christine D. Pohl, *Making Room: Recovering Hospitality as a Christian Tradition* (Grand Rapids, MI: Eerdmans, 1999), 44, quoting Julian, "Letter 22," ed. W. C. Wright, in *The Works of the Emperor Julian*, Loeb Classical Library (New York: Putnam, 1953), I:58–70.

2. Duane Litfin, *Word Versus Deed: Resetting the Scales to a Biblical Balance* (Wheaton, IL: Crossway, 2012), 63.

3. Chris began using the term "apologetic of mercy" in 2008 in papers he wrote as a student at Reformed Theological Seminary.

Chapter 1: Tangible Grace

1. Frederick Dale Bruner, *Matthew: A Commentary* (Grand Rapids, MI: Eerdmans, 2004), 569.

2. See Luke 24:19. Also see chapters 2–8 of Acts, where Luke describes how both word and deed were prominent in the ministry of the apostles.

3. See John 5:1-14, where Jesus tells a man He had healed of paralysis to "sin no more." We do not know what sins he was guilty of, but Jesus clearly says the man needed both physical and spiritual healing. He also had relational problems, because he had no one to help him get into the pool. And we can safely

assume the man had emotional scars after being paralyzed for thirty-eight years.

4. Another example is found in Joel 3:16-17: "But the LORD is a refuge to his people, a stronghold to the people of Israel. So you shall know that I am the LORD your God." The word *so* indicates that the knowledge results from God being a "refuge" and a "stronghold" for His needy people.

5. See John 12:37-38 and also John 6:26-63, where Jesus teaches that material assistance (earthly bread) is insufficient. All human beings need the Bread of Life—Jesus Himself—more than anything else.

Chapter 2: Tell *and* Show: Deeds Authenticate the Message

1. Blake Williams, phone interview with author, March 6, 2013.

2. Look at John 1:46, where Philip simply told skeptical Nathanael, "Come and see."

3. See Exodus 3:8; 6:6; 1 Samuel 17:37; 2 Kings 20:6; Psalm 18:16-19; 107:19-20; 116:1-8; 2 Corinthians 1:8-10; 2 Peter 2:9.

4. Douglas Groothuis, *Christian Apologetics: A Comprehensive Case for Biblical Faith* (Downers Grove, IL: InterVarsity, 2011), 24.

5. See John 20:30-31.

6. Francis A. Schaeffer, *The God Who Is There* (Downers Grove, IL: InterVarsity, 1998), 185.

7. Bruce Marshall, *The World, the Flesh, and Father Smith* (Boston: Houghton Mifflin, 1945), 108.

8. See also John 17:20-23.

9. John Calvin, *Institutes of the Christian Religion*, III.2.36. Full quote: "For the Word of God is not received by faith if it flits about in the top of the brain, but when it takes root in the depth of the heart . . . *the heart's distrust is greater than the mind's blindness.* It is harder for the heart to be furnished with

assurance [of God's love] than for the mind to be endowed with thought."

Chapter 3: Show *and* Tell: Words Articulate the Message

1. I heard this from Fred Harrell, pastor of City Church in San Francisco, which calls its members "to be stewards of their power and gifts for the honor of Christ and the benefit of urban communities." City Church members spend time with needy people in jail, homeless shelters, hospice, and public schools.

2. I am not saying that deeds don't communicate anything. They can communicate the compassion and character of God. (See chapter 6.) However, while your deeds are the *fruit* of the gospel, they do not communicate the *content* of the gospel. The Social Gospel's problem was the assertion that every soul has already been saved through Christ's sacrifice, and the role of the church is to inform everyone of a salvation they already have by making it manifest in material ways. While Scripture clearly contradicts this view, it also states clearly that the gospel will have social impact.

3. If you struggle with the idea of hell and find it hard to believe a loving God would send anyone there, I encourage you to read *Hell Is Real (But I Hate to Admit It)* by Brian Jones (Colorado Springs, CO: David C Cook, 2011), as well as *Erasing Hell* by Francis Chan and Preston Sprinkle (Colorado Springs, CO: David C Cook, 2011).

4. You may have heard the following quote, attributed to Saint Francis: "Preach the gospel at all times. Use words if necessary." Well, he didn't say it, and it doesn't make much sense anyway. Word and deed are not interchangeable. Jesus preached the gospel with words—and He used deeds to authenticate His identity. See *Francis of Assisi and His World* by Mark Galli (Downers Grove, IL: InterVarsity, 2003) and *Word Versus Deed* by Duane Litfin (Wheaton, IL: Crossway, 2012).

5. See Leviticus 19:18; Isaiah 58; Ezekiel 16:49-50; Micah 6; Matthew 19:19; 22:34-40; Luke 6:27; Romans 13:8-10; 15:2; Colossians 3:12-14; James 2:8.

6. Musicians sometimes deflect praise as well. Johann Sebastian Bach, one of the world's greatest composers, always wrote "S.D.G." at the end of his compositions. Soli Deo Gloria means "to God alone be the glory."

7. Oswald Chambers, *My Utmost for His Highest* (Grand Rapids, MI: Discovery House Publishers, 2008), October 26 entry.

Chapter 4: The Credibility of Love

1. Maya Angelou, *I Know Why the Caged Bird Sings* (New York: Random House, 1969), 23.

2. See orphancareresources.org, ecpat.net, unicef.org.

3. Many people have been disappointed by love. They have heard the words "I love you" but saw deeds that contradicted the words. Human love disappoints us and cannot define love. Hallmark cards and Hollywood do not define love. God created love, and He defines it for us. He shows us what love is by actually loving us. God's love is best understood through the lens of the cross: "This is love: not that we loved God, but that he loved us and sent his Son as an atoning sacrifice for our sins" (1 John 4:10, NIV).

4. See 1 Peter 2:12; Philippians 4:5; Colossians 4:5; 1 Thessalonians 4:11-12; 2 Corinthians 9:13.

5. See Isaiah 58:7-11; Nehemiah 5:10-12; Philippians 2:3-4; Ephesians 4:29-32.

6. *Merriam-Webster's Collegiate Dictionary*, 11th edition, s.v. "altruism."

7. I found the term *alien altruism* in Colin Grant's book *Altruism and Christian Ethics* (Cambridge: Cambridge University Press, 2004).

8. Robert George, "A Clash of Orthodoxies: An Exchange," *First Things* 104 (June/July 2000), 51.

9. Richard Dawkins, *The Selfish Gene* (London: Granada, 1978), 8.

10. "Essentials of Objectivism," Ayn Rand Institute, http://www.aynrand.org/site/PageServer?pagename=objectivism_essentials, accessed May 7, 2013.

11. Charles Darwin wrote that evidence for true other-centeredness would "annihilate my theory, for such could not have been produced by natural selection," in *On the Origin of Species by Means of Natural Selection, or The Preservation of Favored Races in the Struggle for Life* (Cambridge, MA: Harvard University Press, 1967), 199.

12. Alister McGrath wrote, "Is morality dependent upon a transcendent norm or ground—such as God? In debate, many atheists dismiss this question as ridiculous. How dare anyone suggest that atheists are immoral because they do not believe in God! But that is not the real issue. The big question is whether an objective morality can be sustained without belief in God. For Christians, God alone offers an objective foundation for moral values, which is not subject to the whims of the powerful or the changing moods of public opinion," in *Mere Apologetics: How to Help Seekers and Skeptics Find Faith* (London: Baker, 2012), 105.

13. In Isaiah 58 we learn that God's litmus test for true faith is this: *Do you give to those who can never pay you back?* It's the same thing James said: "Religion that God our Father accepts as pure and faultless is this: to look after orphans and widows in their distress and to keep oneself from being polluted by the world" (James 1:27, NIV). See also Deuteronomy 10:18; 24:17; Jeremiah 7:6; Zechariah 7:10. It is altruistic to care for the widows, the fatherless, and the foreigner among us. These were the three categories of Israelites who could not own land, who

had no direct access to the riches of the land of milk and honey. They were dependent on farmers who left crops in the field for them to glean. They could not repay the generous gifts they received, which is why giving to them was truly altruistic.

14. Bryan Follis, *Truth with Love: The Apologetics of Francis Schaeffer* (Wheaton, IL: Crossway, 2006), 137.

15. Blaise Pascal, *Pensées* (Mineola, NY: Dover Publications, 2003), 52.

Chapter 5: The Cause of Suffering

1. See Mark 16:16; Colossians 1:21-23.

2. Thomas Watson, "Man's Misery by the Fall," in *Body of Divinity: Contained in Sermons upon the Assembly's Catechism* (Whitefish, MT: Kessinger Publishing, 2006), 106.

3. C. S. Lewis, *Mere Christianity* (New York: Touchstone Books, 1996), 38.

4. C. S. Lewis, *The Problem of Pain* (London: HarperCollins, 2002), 91.

5. See Genesis 2:16-17; 3:16-19; Romans 5:12-21; 8:20-22; 1 Corinthians 15:21-22.

6. See Romans 1:16; Galatians 1:6-9; 1 Corinthians 15:1-2; 2 Corinthians 11:3-4.

7. Methodist missionary E. Stanley Jones said about separating word and deed ministry, "The social gospel divorced from personal salvation is like a body without a soul. The message of personal salvation without a social dimension is like a soul without a body. The former is a corpse, the latter is a ghost." Quoted in Donald Atkinson and Charles Roesel, *Meeting Needs, Sharing Christ* (Nashville: LifeWay, 1995), 26.

8. Of course, that man's paralysis was not caused by his own sin, but by original sin. It's an important distinction, because we don't want to blame someone for suffering he or she did not cause.

See John 9, where the disciples assume a blind man or his parents must be to blame for the man's blindness.

9. See James 4:14; Psalm 102:3; Job 7:7.

10. Richard Stengel, "Apostle of Sunny Thoughts," *Time* (March 18, 1985), 70.

Part 2: The Apologetic of Mercy: *How*

1. Emmanuel Suhard (1874–1949) was a French cardinal of the Roman Catholic Church. Quoted in Eugene Peterson, *Practice Resurrection* (Grand Rapids, MI: Eerdmans, 2010), 185.

Chapter 6: Names

1. Augustine, *Lectures on the Gospel of John*, chapter 13 paragraph 5.

2. The International Labor Organization estimates there are 21 million slaves in the world today. The Carr Center for Human Rights Policy at Harvard puts the number at 29 million or more. See the Resources section for more on slavery and human trafficking.

3. Story provided to me by International Justice Mission, with the woman's name changed for her protection.

4. Find the full list on my website, http://tangibletheology.com/resources/names-list/.

5. It's often rendered as *Lord* in the English Bible, but the literal Hebrew is *I Am*.

6. Roy and Revel Hession, *We Would See Jesus* (Fort Washington, PA: CLC Publications, 1958), 40–43.

7. See Hebrews 4:6-11 for more on the connection between the ministries of Joshua and Jesus.

8. Cornelius Plantinga Jr., *Engaging God's World: A Christian Vision of Faith, Learning, and Living* (Grand Rapids, MI: Eerdmans, 2002), 80.

9. This phrase comes from Bruce K. Waltke and Charles Yu, *An Old Testament Theology: An Exegetical, Canonical, and Thematic Approach* (Grand Rapids, MI: Zondervan, 2007), 365.

Chapter 7: Presence

1. According to the Center for the Study of Global Christianity at Gordon-Conwell Theological Seminary. See http://www.gordonconwell.edu/resources/documents/StatusOfGlobal Mission.pdf.

2. Frank J. Cunningham, ed., *Words to Love By: Mother Teresa* (Notre Dame, IN: Ave Maria Press, 1983), 27.

3. The *Jesus* film, based on the gospel of Luke, is available in more than 1,100 languages. See www.jesusfilm.org.

4. Lon Solomon, "It's All About the Resurrection," sermon preached at McLean Bible Church, McLean, VA, July 11, 2004, http://www.mcleanbible.org/pages/page.asp?page_id=83820#.

5. See Daniel 3:25.

Chapter 8: Proactivity

1. John Piper, "Jesus Is the End of Ethnocentrism," sermon preached on Luke 4:16-30, January 20, 2002, http://www.desiringgod.org/ResourceLibrary/TopicIndex/48/81_Jesus_Is_the_End_of_Ethnocentrism/.

2. John Calvin, *Institutes of the Christian Religion*, 1.13.1.

3. Notice this: The people did *nothing* to deserve help! The word *therefore* does not refer to repentance or anything the people did. Instead, God "allures" them out of their sinful state, using mercy and love, into relationship with Him.

4. Paul Miller, *Love Walked Among Us: Learning to Love Like Jesus* (Colorado Springs, CO: NavPress, 2001), 23.

5. Art Lindsley, *Love, the Ultimate Apologetic*, (Downer's Grove, IL: InterVarsity, 2008), 88.

6. "*Agape* (love) seems to have been virtually a Christian invention—a new word for a new thing (apart from about twenty occurrences in the Greek version of the Old Testament, it is almost non-existent before the New Testament). Agape draws its meaning directly from the revelation of God in Christ. It is not a form of natural affection, however intense, but a supernatural fruit of the Spirit (Gal. 5:22). It is a matter of will rather than feeling (for Christians must love even those they dislike—Matt. 5:44-48). It is the basic element in Christlikeness." J. I. Packer, *Your Father Loves You* (Wheaton, IL: Harold Shaw Publishers, 1986), devotional entry for March 10.

Chapter 9: Yes, You

1. Lane T. Dennis, ed., *Letters of Francis A. Schaeffer* (Westchester, IL: Crossway, 1985), 63.
2. See 1 Corinthians 3:5-9.
3. See Luke 8:16; 11:33. Look also at the story of the Good Samaritan in Luke 10:25-37. The priest and the Levite were too busy doing their jobs and too concerned for their own safety to show compassion.
4. "We live in a time and place where, over and over, when confronted with something unpleasant we pursue not coping but overcoming. Often we succeed. Most of humanity has not enjoyed and does not enjoy such luxury. Death shatters our illusion that we can make do without coping. When we have overcome absence with phone calls, winglessness with airplanes, summer heat with air-conditioning—when we have overcome all these and more besides, then there will abide two things with which we must cope: the evil in our hearts and death." Nicholas Wolterstorff, *Lament for a Son* (Grand Rapids, MI: Eerdmans, 1987), 72–73.
5. See Exodus 16:1-36; Numbers 11:1-9.

6. C. H. Spurgeon, *The Gospel of the Kingdom: A Popular Exposition of the Gospel According to Matthew* (New York: Baker & Taylor, 1893), 222.

Chapter 10: Abiding

1. In a similar way, Peter spoke for the disciples in John 6:68: "Lord, to whom shall we go? You have the words of eternal life." Despite their bewilderment over the things they had heard about eating Jesus' flesh and drinking His blood, those men knew there was nowhere else they could go but to the Truth.
2. See John 7:27; Isaiah 55:1-3.
3. Read John 21 and notice that Jesus prepared breakfast and fed Peter before He told Peter to "Feed my sheep." I also find it intriguing that Jesus took the time to cook for His disciples and eat with them as one of the last things He did before ascending to heaven.
4. John Piper, *Don't Waste Your Cancer* (Wheaton, IL: Crossway, 2011). The book came out of an article Piper wrote in 2006, which includes helpful comments from David Powlison of the Christian Counseling and Education Foundation. You can find the article at http://www.desiringgod.org/resource-library/taste-see-articles/dont-waste-your-cancer.
5. Piper, *Don't Waste Your Cancer*, 10.
6. Piper, *Don't Waste Your Cancer*, 11.
7. Dan B. Allender, *Leading with a Limp: Take Full Advantage of Your Most Powerful Weakness* (Colorado Springs, CO: WaterBrook Press, 2006).

Conclusion

1. When Jesus sent the disciples out to do ministry, He expected them to employ both word and deed. See Matthew 10:7-8; Luke 10:9.

2. See Galatians 3:7,29; Ephesians 3:1-6.
3. See Matthew 4:23; 9:35. Later, Philip also "preached good news about the kingdom of God" (Acts 8:12).
4. Jürgen Moltmann, *The Way of Jesus Christ: Christology in Messianic Dimensions* (London: SCM, 1990), 98–99.
5. *Biblical Guidelines for Mercy Ministry in the Presbyterian Church in America* (15th General Assembly, 1987), Appendix T, 506–514.

ABOUT THE AUTHOR

Once an adamant atheist, Chris Sicks now serves as Pastor of Mercy at Alexandria Presbyterian Church in Virginia. Previously he was a deacon and Director of Mercy Ministry at the church. He has worked at a homeless shelter and drug recovery program in Washington, DC, and served as executive director of a mentoring and scholarship program for DC children.

Chris is a member of the Christian Community Development Association (CCDA) and Evangelicals for Social Action. He leads periodic workshops on mercy ministry for CCDA and the Presbyterian Church in America.

Prior to ministry, Chris was an army officer, a restaurant manager, and a journalist with more than one thousand newspaper stories and weekly columns published. He and his wife, Sara, live in Northern Virginia with their three children.